WITH MALICE TOWARDS NONE

JAMES M. HARE

WITH MALICE

TOWARDS NONE:

The Musings of
A Retired Politician

WITH A FOREWORD BY RUSSEL B. NYE

MICHIGAN STATE UNIVERSITY PRESS

1972

★
★
★
★
★

Contents

FOREWORD   vii

PREFACE   ix

    I.   THE GREATEST PROBLEM   1

   II.   THE LABOR MOVEMENT   12

  III.   THE LEGAL FRATERNITY   24

  IV.   THE GRAND JURIES *vs* THE OMBUDSMAN   44

   V.   THE LOBBYIST   56

  VI.   PATRONAGE—POLITICAL OR OTHERWISE   68

 VII.   THE SLUSH FUNDS   83

VIII.   THE NEWS MEDIA   88

  IX.   PUBLIC DISCLOSURE   92

   X.   PRIVACY OR CONCEALMENT   102

  XI.   ECONOMY AND EFFICIENCY   108

 XII.   CAMPAIGN FUNDS   117

XIII.   THE CAMPAIGN TRAIL   126

XIV.   THE RECURRING QUESTIONS   134

 XV.   TRAFFIC SAFETY   138

XVI.   THE M.V.A.C.F.   151

XVII.   THE LIGHTER SIDE   164

XVIII.   WE ALL MAKE MISTAKES   169

XIX.   MICHIGAN DEMOCRATS: WHY DO THEY LOSE?   175

 XX.   I REST MY CASE   193

A Note of Thanks   196

"Politics is a refined form of cannibalism and men will flow to and support any form of government or political party that enriches them in power, prestige and money, regardless of its goals and morals."

Anon.

Foreword

One of the first great pragmatists of American politics, Mark Hanna, once said of it, "Don't expect too much of human nature." On the other hand, it was Will Rogers, another realistic commentator on the American scene, who remarked that, given the political system we have and the politicians who run it, both work out better than you'd expect.

Jim Hare's reminiscences of Michigan politics (nobody ever called him James) contain something of both viewpoints. He was deeply involved in state politics long enough to know exactly how it worked, and too long to lose faith in the fact that it *does* work. A quarter century of practical, day-to-day experience showed him where the vulnerable joints in the machinery were, and at the same time showed that it kept running fairly well, no matter how inept its operators sometimes were. Familiarity with politics in his case did not breed contempt for the system, nor cynicism, but rather a respectful confidence in it—substituting a few changes here and there, of course, and adding a bit of common sense.

The reader, whether he is a politically-minded partisan or simply an interested spectator, should not expect to find Jim's book a way of paying off old scores, or a gossipy "inside" exposé. It is a reflective book rather than an expository one; it is more even-tempered, one suspects, than were some of the events of which it speaks. There is now and then something between the lines, naturally, but that is not its point.

What the reader finds, first of all, is an account of the apparatus of political life as it is lived in a populous, modern, industrialized state —lobbyists, patronage, campaigns, platforms, promises, money—that underlies the busy but humdrum bureaucratic routine that keeps things like auto licenses going out, fees coming in, and legislators pulling and hauling at a thousand bills a session. More important, one also finds by extension some implications of the Michigan political story that have broader meaning for the citizen who is interested in and concerned about his government. Whether or not the reader agrees with Jim Hare's specific recommendations for political change, he will certainly agree with him that any viable government must change to meet the people's needs, and he will share with him his trust in the American system's ability to do so.

Russel B. Nye

Preface

WHY should a retired Michigan politician write a book? Have not people heard his opinions innumerable times, and have not the news media distributed them far and wide? Is there anything left to say? Are not most books written by retired politicians simply defenses of their own administration? What is the reason for this late inspiration to write? Why didn't the politician say those things that he now wants to say in book form while he was in office? These are good questions. But there is a reason for this book. Primarily because the politician in office is faced with temporary but instant crises which demand his immediate answers. The man in office does not concern himself with long range problems nor long range solutions, thus, the justification for this book.

It is my opinion that the state of Michigan, and particularly the metropolitan cities, are faced with certain overwhelming problems for which we have not been able to find solutions. Indeed, problems such as drug addiction, pollution, poverty and social unrest seem to be growing faster than answers can be found, and the problems not only multiply but proliferate until they become so thoroughly entwined that it is an amorphous enigma most difficult to deal with in a democratic society. I do not propose to indict our political parties for failure in this matter, nor the individual leaders of our state. The political parties are nothing more than debaters in this great social dilemma, and the leaders are so circumscribed by the structure of government that they can only plead, promise and pray for a better day. To ask the leaders in government in this state to remedy the ills is like asking a blacksmith to manufacture a Lincoln Continental. Neither one has the tools to work with. This unfortunate leader group is limited, enclosed and confined by a tight net of constitutional law, tradition and myth. The basics of the constitution which they must live by were written nearly two hundred years ago by a group of rural delegates who had no concept of the changes which would come to this nation.

They had written a document which would protect them from the force and furies of the kings of England, but it does not have relevance to the needs of today when the complexities of Government exceed anything that the constitutional delegates in the 1700's could ever imagine.

I shall offer some rather unorthodox suggestions to combat this dilemma of governmental impotence, but in addition I shall describe, in some detail, the interacting forces which tend to influence government sometimes even more than law. These forces, powerful as they may be in influencing government, I find are little understood by the general public. Such groups as the labor movement, the legal fraternity, lobbyists, recipients of political patronage and the political parties, are a part of what the younger generation calls the Establishment. Our governmental structure has been kind to these factions. It provides a comfortable theatre for these groups and one which they appreciate, and they are not likely to encourage any drastic change; yet, in my opinion, change in the governmental structure is absolutely essential if things are to be done quickly enough to be meaningful. The social problems facing us cannot wait for a long range solution of years and decades. The world moves quickly now. The underprivileged demand instant response. The structure of government is simply not geared to move quickly.

I realize that I move myself to the end of a limb with the prediction that government must reform or perish as a viable entity. The correctness or error of my judgment will soon be apparent. Certainly, if the powers of government, within ten years, cannot at least contain the social unrest, then the forces of violence may well take over. There are a great group of people in this state, particularly in the metropolitan areas, who believe that they are discriminated against. They are a most dissimilar amalgamation and the one thing they have in common is that they feel the government has failed them. Such groups as the Black community, the property taxpayer, the drug addict, the poverty stricken, have one common bond—they are rebelling against their government; and, since it is much easier to destroy than to construct, they can form a common cause against their political leadership.

WITH MALICE TOWARDS NONE

I

MICHIGAN'S GREATEST PROBLEM

THE government of Michigan, because of its structure and its organization, cannot cope with the great problems that face it. These are strong and harsh words, coupled with a dismal opinion. They are not the words that I would have uttered when I first came into state government in the early nineteen fifties, but after twenty years of watching the frustrations of the leaders of our state, I have come to the conclusion that we have an unworkable situation to deal with. This is not a criticism of either political party, nor of the leaders of those parties. Indeed, I have worked with four governors over a period of twenty years, and each of them tried hard and diligently to deal with the problems that were building up. Unfortunately, they were unable to cope with most problems and the situation has deteriorated. Over the last two or three years, I have reached the conclusion that, because of the constitutional structure of the state, our government simply cannot function effectively to correct the problems that surround us.

Let me trace those events which brought me to this unhappy conclusion. For some years I had the privilege of working with high school graduates attending a series of seminars under the direction of D. Hale Brake, a former (the twelve years prior to 1955) State Treasurer of Michigan. Mr. Brake brought together high school graduates who were of unusual caliber and intelligence, gathered them into a central location and subjected them to meetings with state, county and local officials. In this way they learned the views of those officials on the problems of the day. In the course of this seminar experience, these high school graduates made a list of what they considered to be the great and outstanding problems of their particular year. This list, as you would suspect, changed over the course of time. There were such matters as penal reform, unemployment, traffic safety, pollution, ecology control, divorce laws, the eighteen year old vote, discrimination, equality between the races, educational reform, drug addiction, and inflation, to name just a few of the subjects which interested them.

Over the years the discussions in these seminars were based upon a belief that state and local governments could, in time, meet and solve all these problems. No one seemed to recognize that they would not and could not. It was not until the revolt of youth began that I started to understand this fact—seeing, as one did, the unrest on the campuses of the universities, in the high schools, and in the ghettos of our cities.

In all these seminars no one brought forward the fact that the greatest problem in state government was to make that government function. You may think that it does function; that our legislatures pass literally hundreds of laws in a session; and that hundreds of millions of dollars are regularly appropriated for good purposes. Yet, it is my opinion that, no matter how well we are doing, our problems are growing faster and we are continually finding solutions to problems that are at least ten years out of date. In other words, we enact a solution in 1970 to a problem which should have been solved in 1960.

Let me give you an example. In 1956, I made a tour, with numerous other state and county government officials, to the downriver communities south of Detroit, including Ecorse, Wyandotte, Trenton and Gibralter. We visited the industrial complexes and steel mills. One of the local problems was the very unpleasant, noxious fumes which came from the steel plants, particularly, and not only polluted the air but took the paint off the houses and automobiles.

One morning I had breakfast with the plant manager of one of the steel plants. He laid it on the line for me. He said, "I know how bad these fumes are. I have to live in this community and my wife complains about it all the time. Our company knows that we probably could control most of these fumes with an expenditure of about fourteen or fifteen million dollars over a period of two years. However, if we did so, our plant would show a substantial loss for that two year period, and if we raised our prices enough to pay for it, the mills operating less than fifty miles away around Toledo, that did not have to make this same expenditure, would underbid us on the open market, and we would be closed down. Therefore, I am very honestly going to recommend to management that we work slowly and carefully on this problem, but not to the extent we become economically non-competitive with our competitors in Ohio." Here was an honest man speaking very realistically. In essence neither he nor his company were going to do very much about the problem until they and their competitors in the economic system were forced to.

But starting with that year, and continuing every year thereafter, there have been numerous bills introduced, without a great deal of support, to do something about controlling noxious fumes from the big industrial plants. And year after year they became buried in committee. Very often they were buried in committee with the tacit support of the legislators from those districts. Why? Because those legislators feared just what that plant manager had told me—if they became non-competitive the plant in their district would shut down and they would have unemployment in the region.

Now who can you hold responsible for that kind of a situation developing? The Governor? No, because two governors made real efforts to clean up the situation. The Legislature? Yes, to a degree. But it is totally impossible to pinpoint who watered down various bills or, indeed, let them die in committee. Thus, we come to the crux of our governmental failures. How are we ever able to place responsibility on the persons within a state government who cause a program or a bill to live or die?

Certainly you cannot blame any one of the three major branches of government, the executive, judicial, or legislative, for any shortcomings, since none of the three has ever had the authority to put through a reform, or to pass a law, alone. It is a collective action calling for all three of them to deal with the problems of the day.

The Governor can initiate a bill, he can fight for it, and indeed he can veto a bill that he is opposed to. The Legislature can initiate bills, can amend them, and can pass them, subject to the veto of the Governor or the interpretation of the courts. The courts, of course, by their interpretation of law, can change procedures, but they can hardly initiate truly new law. These are the "Checks and Balances" of the American system, and are looked upon as of the utmost importance. They protect the American people from any kind of individual despotism but they do create a situation in which any one of the three branches can effectively veto the action of the other two, and they give great power to those people who do not want to make any change at all. *Status quo* is very often the winner. This, of course, is one of the major reasons we are unable to come up with solutions to the great problems of our day. It may be argued that this system has been viable and workable for almost two hundred years, but the situation of 1971 is very different from the situation of 1900 or 1840. Government did not play such a huge part in the general life of the citizenry in those days.

To put it another way. What if the General Motors Corporation, instead of having officers and an executive board, were much more democratic and worked within a structure exactly like the constitutional structure of the State of Michigan? I think under those conditions they would put out a new model about every four years, and I suspect that no two fenders would be painted the same color when they came off the assembly line!

Let us consider another aspect, that of the time element involved in getting anything done in state government. To bring about a reform or a major change in government, it usually requires extensive legislation and expensive appropriations of monies. For example, assume that the problem to be dealt with is pollution, which is very much in everyone's mind these days. The usual sequence of events needed to bring about a major reform in this area would take approximately eight years.

In the Year One, the executive office, usually the Governor, would appoint a blue ribbon committee of outstanding citizens to study the problem and to make recommendations. In the Year Two, these recommendations would be looked at and studied by legislative committees and, more importantly, by branches of the executive government that would have to implement them. These people, in turn, would visit other states and other countries and see how they handle this particular problem.

The Years Three, Four and Five would probably be taken up in the legislative process. Bills would be introduced in both houses of the Legislature. The bills would go to the pertinent committees in each house, and probably a separate portion of the bill to the appropriations committees of each house. In other words, the bill would be at the mercy of four committees during the period it is in the Legislature. Any one of the four could effectively end the life of that bill by letting it terminate in their committee. The legislative committees would hold public hearings, would call in for advice the lobbyists from all the interests concerned, and perhaps by the end of the Year Five, a bill will be passed by each of the houses that would not be exactly the same. This would require a conference committee between the two houses. Once again there is a possibility of the bill dying at this point. Hopefully, however, by this time the bill did get to the Governor's desk, he would sign it and give it the force of law.

In the Year Six, the executive areas of the government having responsibility for the new pollution law would begin to implement it. They would move slowly and carefully, first of all because the appropriation of the monies probably would not come to them until the next fiscal year, and, secondly, because they would operate a "pilot" operation for the first year after the law is in effect, for the very good reason that they would know there would be challenges to the new law.

In the Years Seven and Eight the new law would be challenged. The polluters, to whom it may be a very expensive matter to end the pollution, may challenge it on its constitutionality, and those challenges would drag through the courts from the Circuit Court to the Court of Appeals to the Supreme Court, and back down again in all probability, so that those years would be gone before any definite settlement is arrived at as to whether the law shall be effectively enforced, or not. In the Year Nine, if all had gone well during the preceeding Eight, we would probably have a law which would work pretty well, but very likely it would be the law which dealt with the problem in the Year One.

Now I have pointed out two great defects in the constitutional structure of our state government. First the luxury of the "Checks and Balances" system, which does not allow any group, any individual or any branch of government to have enough power to accept responsibility; and, secondly, the "Time Element" that permits a problem to get completely out of hand before a solution can be arrived at and even that solution may be too late for the needs of the problem of that latter day.

The need for very drastic constitutional reforms is apparent. First, I think we need to centralize more power and thereby more responsibility in one of the branches of government. I think that branch should be the executive branch, and the person involved, the governor.

Secondly, speed is essential in the legislative process. We cannot afford the luxury of taking eight years to bring about partial reform. Representative Joe Swallow, of Alpena, has apparently seen the same need and he is proposing we set up in Michigan a unicameral legislature, such as they have in Nebraska. This, to a degree, would bring about two of the reforms needed. His plan would eliminate one house completely, and thereby would eliminate the need for a bill to go to additional committees within that house. This action would probably speed up the passage of necessary reform legislation by about two years. This plan certainly, and he recognizes it full well, has one great weakness. It requires that a goodly number of the present legislators would thereby lose their positions in government, so that inevitably he will have a core of opposition that will be very strong.

I would propose an alternate reform. Namely, that the constitution be changed to allow the governor to initiate legislation, in both houses. If that legislation was not vetoed by three quarters of the members of each house, within a three month period, the governor's bill would have the force of law. This kind of a constitutional change would certainly give the Governor vast powers. He would also have to accept the full responsibility for the bill. But it would insure that a decision would be reached within ninety days, and eliminate many years of strife and turmoil.

I can hear the storm of protest already. Many will argue that a system that has existed for almost two hundred years should not be changed. There will be accusations that I am encouraging a dictatorship. But the one thing I am sure of is that the present system is not working. In my opinion it cannot work, and we must take the bull by the horns and make some rather radical changes in our constitution.

There will be people who will argue that this will stifle debate and the inner-exchange of opinions, and will do away with compromise. There is certainly some truth in that accusation, but in my opinion the virtues of the proposed system are greater than its defects. I think the virtues of compromise are given far too much credit. I have found that they usually mean that a bill gets watered down to the point where it is impotent and does not do the job it was intended to do. Let me give you an example. In 1960, the Secretary of State's office was having a problem with drivers licenses. A substantial number of these were being counterfeited, and sold to the general public by the counterfeiters. It was at this point that I decided to follow the lead of several other states and have a color photograph of the operator appended to the license. There was no real opposition to the idea. The law enforcement bodies recognized that it would stop the exchange of driver licenses between youthful drivers, and help stop the misuse of licenses for purchasing liquor. Furthermore, the new licenses would help the merchants identify people wishing to cash checks. However, when the bill authorizing the use of photographs hit the Legislature, there was a rumble of discontent, and the bill died in committee. After several years the opposition to the bill was pinpointed. We found a substantial group of legislators were opposed to the bill if the negatives of the pictures were kept in State Department files, but if the negatives were destroyed immediately after printing the photograph on the license, they would accept the bill. This was compromise, and it was accepted by myself and by the legislators who favored the bill. However, no other state in the country guaranteed to destroy the negatives after printing the picture. In the other states, the negatives were kept and, if there was a question about the substitution of a bogus picture on a license, the picture could be compared with the original negative. The police departments in other states made substantial use of the negatives in the files of the driver licensing office.

In one tragic case a negative could have been invaluable. The sequence of events was as follows. On Thursday, July 9, 1970, a motorist went to the Quick Title Counter of the Secretary of State's office asking for the immediate issuance of a title on his car. He was agitated and extremely nervous. When told that he had come too late to get the title issued to him that day, he said he absolutely had to have the title in order to sell his car. He had to have money at once. He was told to come back the following morning for his title. At that point he left. However, the clerks who had talked to him were concerned over his actions and his agitation. They feared he was a drug addict and that he was so desperate for money he might return and hold them up.

Meanwhile, minutes after this, a holdup and a kidnapping took place. A robber had gone to a gift shop in Lansing, knocked the store owner, Mrs. Gallagher, unconscious, and kidnapped Laurie Murningham, the daughter of a former Mayor of Lansing. He took her and the proceeds of the cash register to his car.

The Secretary of State's office did not learn of the holdup and kidnapping until late in the night of July 9th. But on July 10th, the motorist who had asked for a Quick Title had come under suspicion. In every way, the description given by Mrs. Gallagher fitted the description of the man who had been at the Secretary of State's office.

Eyewitness accounts of the clothing seen in both places were identical and all agreed that he had a Fu Manchu mustache and a goatee. He became a prime suspect. The police were given the name and addresses used by the suspect for the past six years. But one thing, of course, was missing. Had the police, or the Secretary of State's office, been able to go to their files and select a picture of the suspect, they could then have given it to Mrs. Gallagher for comparison, and a decision could have been reached as to whether or not it was, indeed, the same man. Some days later, the body of Laurie Murningham was found and the charge was changed from kidnapping to murder.

The point that I would make here is that as the result of a legislative compromise, no negatives or pictures of motorists are kept in the files. Had they been, then there would have been a chance for the quick detention of a prime suspect. So far no suspect has been apprehended.

Let me give you yet another example of what can happen to a bill in the legislative labyrinth. Some years ago, following the federal government's recommendations on traffic safety, I decided that we should set up a Medical Review Board, whose function would be to review the medical and mental disabilities of potential drivers. Up to this time, the examiner who passed judgment over a potential driver's capabilities was often in a quandary. With no medical background or psychiatric training, he was hardly in a position, in borderline cases, to decide whether an applicant for a driver's license was a good risk or not. When he had to make his judgment about a person with a cardiac impairment or a vision defect, he could not make a reliable one. The method of handling this situation was to ask the applicant to return to his own family doctor and get a statement as to his condition. Very often the statement that was received from the family doctor was one that said nothing more than: "In my judgment this person is capable of driving." Doctors themselves did not like the position they were put in. Here they were, the family doctors and, all of a sudden, called upon to make a quasi-police judgment that could take their patient off the road.

A better solution was a board of medical experts, who had training in the detection of impediments to good driving. Therefore, I had a bill entered into the legislative hoppers which would set up a seven man medical board. The total cost of the program would have been $20,000, half of which would have been born by the federal government. There was no opposition to it in the legislative channels. I assumed we were away, free and clear, and that the next year we could go into business with the Medical Review Board. Unfortunately, since the bill had to go to two committees in each House, one an Appropriations Committee and one a Highway Traffic Safety Committee, it meant that four committees were involved. Much to my amazement, at the end of that session, I found that, although the bill had passed three of the committees, and the monies appropriated, it had got lost in the legislative logjam at the end of the session and had not been considered by one committee. So it went down the drain for that year.

Fortunately, it worked out fairly well. A number of doctors, working with the State Medical Society, volunteered their services and we got the kind of medical help we wanted—in spite of not having a law on the books that authorized it. This has since been remedied and monies have been appropriated. We are now in the legal business of making medical determinations with competent persons making the decisions.

I hope that I have made a reasonable case that the system of "Checks and Balances" in state government is not working. I cannot believe, for instance, that the educational system is better than it was twenty-five years ago, in spite of the untold millions of dollars poured into it. I cannot believe that the rehabilitation of convicts, or the reform of our penal system, has improved in the last two decades. I cannot believe that we have the drug addiction problem under control. I am not satisfied that the ecology and pollution problem is being solved. In short, for some reason, and in spite of great efforts and untold millions of dollars being appropriated, we do not seem to be gaining.

Personally, I do not blame the people or the political parties involved. I blame the rigid structure of the Constitution, which demands that we continue to have a "Checks and Balances" system. As I have said, the opposition to any change would be very great. And yet I am convinced that the American people, if they realized that we are not making the gains we should, would be amenable to a constitutional change. In a larger perspective, if we look about the world, we see constitutional and democratic governments falling, and being replaced by dictatorships. There must be a middle ground, a compromise between an outright dictatorship and the democratic government we have known for so long.

I think a comparison is in order. The inability of the State of Michigan to solve its basic problems is not unlike the inability of the Weimar Republic to cope with its problems following World War I.

The Michigan problems are those of the present. The Weimar Republic's downfall came in the years 1929 to 1933. Michigan cannot find a suitable solution for such things as pollution, rehabilitation of criminals, carnage on the highways, or campus revolts. Neither could the Weimar Republic find a solution for land reform, unemployment, inflation or reparations payments to the Allied Countries. The net result in both places—great frustration on the part of the people.

This analogy is by no means far-fetched. Just as you had fire bombings, murder and rioting in the streets during the period of the Weimar Republic, so you find these events in Michigan today. These events in Germany killed a democracy and paved the way for the Nazi regime. One of the main German problems was the inflexibility of the Weimar constitution. We have a similar inflexibility but one can only hope that we will not suffer the same consequences and a change can be brought about before events overtake us.

With this impotency in state government, what can the older citizen tell the younger? Up-to-date, mature people have been advising the young people to cease their activist role of confrontation with the Establishment; cease the violence and sit-ins; certainly cease the use of bombs and violence and rioting. Become a part of the government; become involved in campaigns; run for office; and take an active part in the government functions. However, if the weakness of our government is in its rigidity, its constitutionality and thus its inability to cope with problems, then the infusion of new young blood into the government is really not going to be the answer. The young activists feel there is selfishness, incompetence, corruption and indifference in the personnel of government, little recognizing that the rigid structure of our laws and Constitution make it almost impossible to work quickly to correct any great injustices. A few of them will be quick to say that the only answer is revolution. Personally, I cannot believe that violent revolution can, necessarily, bring about an improvement. My moderate opinion will not be believed by the activists and unless we find a way of getting government off dead-center and finding a solution for its rigidity, I feel we are in for a bad time for the foreseeable future.

II

THE LABOR MOVEMENT

A commentary on the political climate of Michigan would not be complete without including the labor movement, particularly as it has affected the Democratic Party. But first a personal reminiscence.

My father disapproved of drinking, smoking and chewing gum because they were pleasurable. He strongly disapproved of the Democratic Party and the union movement and he feared the Catholic Church. In short, I am the product of a WASP culture (white, anglo-saxon protestant). When I told my father at age twenty-one that I was a Democrat and that I favored the union movement, he was aghast, to put it mildly. Nevertheless, when I graduated from college in 1932, he secured a job for me in the Ford Foundry, even though it was in the depths of the depression. That job lasted only ten weeks but certainly made me far more sympathetic to the need for a union at the Ford Motor Company. The stifling heat around the blast furnaces, the grit and dirt of the foundry sand and the seemingly total indifference about working conditions on the part of supervisory employees made me feel something was decidedly wrong. This, of course, was five years before the UAW was able to organize the Ford Motor Company. I remember how my services were terminated in the tenth week. I was sitting on the floor of the foundry eating my lunch when my boss came by and said, "You're all through at 4 o'clock." Nothing more, nothing less. I must admit, in defense of the supervisory personnel at Ford, they were under great pressure to cut costs and the company was losing a million dollars a day.

Some years later, after I became a teacher, I was an active officer in the Detroit Federation of Teachers. Still later, I became a delegate to the AFL's Wayne County Central Labor body. By the middle of the 1940's, I was a committed supporter of the labor movement and knowledgeable about the workings of the union organization.

At the close of World War II, the National ADA (Americans for Democratic Action) was formed in about twenty-five states in the country. It was strictly an anti-communist organization and all members had to sign an affidavit stating they were not communists. In general, the ADA represented the non-communist left in the thinking of the liberals. I became the first chairman of the Detroit Chapter and continued as such for three years. I worked very closely with the labor movement and particularly with the UAW in Detroit. The UAW was beginning to test its political strength. The catalyst which brought together the various elements of the labor movement, the nationality groups and the black community, was G. Mennen Williams when he ran for governor in 1948.

The 1946 election had been a disaster throughout the state of Michigan for the Democrats. They had lost several offices in Detroit, but by the mid-year 1948, Williams had pulled together a team that did yeoman service. He was able, with the help of Hicks Griffiths, Martha Griffiths, Horace Gilmore, James Lincoln and the Reuther brothers, Frank Martell of the AFL and the leaders of the black community, to take control of the Democratic Party. Hicks Griffiths was named the Democratic State Chairman. This was the first time the UAW committed its entire state-wide resources to the support of a political candidate. They chose to support G. Mennen Williams in the gubernatorial primary of 1948 against two other more conservative but better known Democrats. With their help, Williams won that primary and overwhelmed Governor Kim Sigler who was up for re-election.

From this point on, the labor movement and particularly the UAW became the single most dominant force in the Democratic Party. Their successes in the beginning were astronomical. Williams won six consecutive terms. A State Administrative Board consisting of Governor, Lieutenant Governor, Secretary of State, Attorney General, State Treasurer, Highway Commissioner and Superintendent of Public Instruction were elected—all Democrats. The Democrats also had a majority in the Legislature. During the late 1940's, I was also the Treasurer of the Fifteenth Congressional District Democratic Organization, and as such had the fund raising chores of the district, as well as the disbursement of funds. One of my duties in election year was to use the money given to the district by the labor movement to pay election-day workers. I soon found that they were most generous in their support. Most of these election-day workers were union members who had taken a day off from their job to enjoy the conviviality and fun of an election day, while being paid for their duties.

During the years of Governor Williams' incumbency, 1949 to 1960, the UAW solidified its strong position with the Democratic Party and by the late 1950's practically any knowledgeable person active in the party knew that the blessing of the UAW was essential for any successful state-wide candidacy. The common saying around the political halls was that the UAW cannot always guarantee that you will win an election against a Republican, but they could control a candidate's bid for nomination either in a Democratic state-wide convention or in a state-wide primary race. They were particularly successful in state-wide primaries. Since primaries ordinarily attract from one-fourth to one-third as many people as turn out for the election, a relatively small group of dedicated workers such as the UAW had, could turn the tide in favor of their candidate. This I learned, to my sorrow, in 1960 when I was a gubernatorial candidate in the Democratic primary. They were equally successful in the Democratic conventions to select the state officers who were going to run for state-wide office. I do not remember a single candidate being nominated in the Democratic convention who was opposed by the UAW. Admittedly some were nominated whom the UAW was indifferent to, but not actively opposed to.

To the average non-union citizen, the term labor movement connotes a vast monolithic organization of great power. The power is there but it is hardly a monolithic organization. There are two large individual unions involved and a third and even fourth section which have often separate goals and intents. First there are the Teamsters, who are independent. Secondly, the UAW, which is now an independent union since its break with the national AFL-CIO when Walter Reuther had a difference of opinion with President George Meany. The third group is the conglomoration group. The state AFL-CIO, for many years under the presidency of Gus Scholle, is a diverse coalition of unions including the Steelworkers and Ironworkers, Retail Clerks, Building Trades, Governmental Employees and the Rubberworkers. At times, there is considerable strife between these groups concerning the political candidates they will support and finance. The Building Trades will sometimes support Republicans for local office, although they usually go along with the Democrats on state and national offices. But within the Democratic Party the single independent union, the UAW, is by far the dominant one, even though an occasional argument takes place between the union, the Building Trades or the state CIO. A good example of this internal strife surfaced at the Democratic state-wide convention in August of 1970, when candidates for State Boards of Education were nominated. The fight between the components of the labor unions was reported on August 27, 1970, by the *Jackson Citizen Patriot* with the headline "Firm Hand of UAW Seen in Democratic Nominations." Here is the story:

> LANSING—United Automobile Workers Union played an overriding role in the dumping of one incumbent education board member and the controversial retention of two others on the state Democratic ticket.
> Dr. Peter Oppewall, State Board of Education president from Grand Rapids, failed to win renomination at the state Democratic convention last weekend after the UAW backed Mrs. Annetta Miller of Huntington Woods.
> At the same time, the UAW was instrumental in squeezing out the renomination of another board incumbent, Thomas J. Brennan of Dearborn and of Don Stevens of Okemos for the

Michigan State University Board of Trustees.

One of the untold stories of the Democratic convention was the final break between Stevens, MSU board chairman, and the Michigan AFL-CIO union for which he had been a staff worker for 24 years. State AFL-CIO President August (Gus) Scholle and Secretary Treasurer William C. Marshall did not work for Stevens' renomination, but the bigger and more powerful UAW forces did.

Stevens resigned recently as AFL-CIO education director, without announcing it publicly, after stating publicly he would return to Michigan and the AFL-CIO. He has been directing a labor program sponsored by the US Office of Economic Opportunity at the University of Minnesota. Reportedly he will take other employment soon, but he could not be reached for comment.

The UAW rejected endorsement of Oppewall partly because of two factors: considerable opposition to his pro-parochiaid views, and the failure of his own home district caucus to support him at first.

Both Oppewall and Brennan haven't made a secret of their parochiaid sentiments, but the matter has never become part of formal State Board of Education policies. It has been a behind-the-scenes ingredient, however, in such matters as the resignation of Dr. Ira Polley, a former state superintendent of public instruction who opposed such help to nonpublic schools.

The Democratic State Central Committee officially took a stand against parochiaid and Oppewall and Brennan's opposite, though quiet, view angered a number of party leaders and rank-and-file members.

Oppewall further got himself in trouble by not doing enough fence-mending with his local party organizations. Much of the problem apparently stemmed from his candidacy as a pro-Robert Kennedy delegate to the 1968 national convention, while the majority of his 5th district (Kent and Ionia Counties) caucus wanted Hubert Humphrey.

Since that period, Oppewall began getting local criticism and didn't keep in close enough contact with district party leaders, in their opinion. The 5th District caucus eventually did give Oppewall almost unanimous support, but by then the UAW had already passed the word to drop him.

Oppewall also lost what could have been a valuable ally at the convention when Ken Robinson, a highly respected UAW regional director, had to miss the meeting to undergo open heart surgery in Texas.

Brennan managed to escape the same fate in spite of his parochiaid feelings chiefly because he has a strong pro-labor record. He has been at odds with some AFL-CIO officers, but the now-separate UAW has kept him in its favor. . . .

As this newspaper story indicates, the UAW almost inevitably wins the internal battles within the labor movement or political battles within the Democratic Party. When the UAW supports and elects a candidate they expect, as is their due, that he will give them substantial loyalty and that he will not oppose them on any policy matter on which labor has taken a stand. The viewpoint of the union is understandable since they contribute a great deal of money to a campaign, elicit worker support for their candidate and, in general, counsel and advise him about the conduct of his campaign. However, some candidates and elected officials rebel against what they consider to be high-handed union domination and when they rebel, of course, there is a clash between that candidate and the union involved. I can remember only one UAW defeat arising from this kind of situation. Some years ago, they decided to purge about a dozen of the Democratic legislators who were not going along with their policies. This purge did not work out at all from the standpoint of the UAW, since these candidates were people who had been in office for several years and had built up a constituency of their own. The majority of them, including E. D. O'Brien, an outspoken Representative from the east side of Detroit, and Senator Michael O'Brien, were among those who fought the purge. One of the interesting by-plays which occurred in this battle was that as soon as the union had publicly announced they were going to purge these individuals, the Teamsters Union immediately gave them active support.

As I worked with the leaders of the various unions I could not help but have great respect for their leadership. I often wondered if the corporations they worked for early in their careers recognized that they had such potential leadership material, probably on an assembly line, twenty-five years ago. If the corporations had enrolled these same people in a management trainee program, they would possibly be among the corporation executives rather than the union leaders. At times, I had differences of opinion with some of these leaders, particularly in the choice of candidates for various offices, but I always thought of them as being hard working, intelligent and dedicated people. Just to name a few who stand out in my mind, there were the three Reuther brothers, Walter, Vic and Roy; Leonard Woodcock, now President of the UAW; Kenneth Morris, Bard Young and Douglas Fraser who are Regional Chiefs; the late Senator Patrick McNamara from the AFL; Herschel Womack of the Retail Clerks; Stan Arnold and Frederick Harris of the Building Trades Union; and Charles Younglove, President of the Steelworkers. Lest I be accused of male chauvinism, I must include the four women presidents of the Detroit Federation of Teachers over a period of more than thirty-five years—Frances Comfort, Florence Sweeney, Antoinette Kolar and Mary Ellen Riordan, the present executive.

In politics, the UAW atempts to keep a low profile. They will vehemently deny that they are the dominant power in the Democratic Party. Indeed, they will try to convey the impression that they are only rank-and-file members working within the party. This public relations position, of course, is good business from their standpoint. They well recognize that most independent citizens, after a strike, take a dim view of all unions and the UAW does not want that viewpoint to rub off in an election in which they are interested. Another very interesting aspect of the labor movement is the actions and viewpoint of the rank-and-file members. Most of them are deeply committed to their union on matters affecting wages, hours or working conditions, and as a strike period approaches there is a rise in the morale of the workers, particularly in the more monotonous jobs. It is a kind of seasonal social activity for many of them, and you hear them at a union meeting say "only two weeks or three weeks more to work and then we will have some fun on the picket line." One very sad commentary, and I can understand how it comes about, is the antagonism the average union member working on a monotonous job feels towards the management. He detests the job, and this carries over to his employer. Personally, having worked on an assembly line only ten weeks in my life, I am hardly an authority on the situation, but I certainly came to detest my job because of the terrible monotony. I have often wondered if the unions, when they came to their annual negotiations for a new contract, would give some consideration to the problems of working conditions and less to the problems of hours and wages. I have an unorthodox suggestion to improve the monotony of working conditions: Have the unions demand that all vice presidents and higher be made to work one day a week on an assembly line of the union's choice. I am sure that working conditions would be improved before too long.

The power of the unions in the Democratic Party is, of course, closely tied to the financial assistance which they can give the party and its candidates. The unions contributed almost two hundred thousand dollars to Sander Levin's campaign in the 1970 gubernatorial race. This amount does not include the support of the local union newspapers and the amount of manpower for campaigning on the streets on election day. Keeping in mind that this was only one candidate and one campaign, you must recognize the tremendous effect of the labor movement on the party when you consider that they are supporting literally dozens of other campaigns and candidates in the same year.

But the amounts of money and campaign support donated to an election are not the only reason the unions are very powerful in the Democratic Party. The other ingredient is their careful and precise planning for a convention. The state-wide Democratic conventions are usually held twice a year and nominations are worked out during those sessions. The individual unions make sure that the delegates to the state convention who are union members get to that convention and, if necessary, pay their expenses during the usual two day period. Once the delegates from the labor movement get to the convention, notices are posted in the lobbies of the hotels telling them where the labor caucuses will be held. It is in these caucuses, usually very late in the evening, that the decisions as to whom will be supported are made. Union delegates are also concerned about the choice of officers of the Democratic Party and particularly the state chairman. Since 1948, no state chairman has been elected who was not accepted by labor: Hicks Griffiths in 1949; Neil Staebler in 1950; Joseph Collins in 1961; Zolton Ferency in 1963; Sander Levin in 1967; and James McNeely in 1969.

Examples of labor's influence in not only the selection of Democratic state chairmen but also in their removal were evidenced in the election of Zolton Ferency in 1963 over incumbent Joseph Collins. A quarrel between labor and Collins over the conduct of the 1962 campaign, in which John Swainson lost in his bid for re-election as governor, resulted in labor opposing Collins for state chairman in February of 1963. In 1967, when Zolton Ferency incurred the wrath of the party leadership because of his opposition to President Johnson and his dovish stand on Vietnam, it was labor once again who provided the muscle in successfully obtaining Ferency's resignation.

In the 1969 election for Democratic state chairman, labor for the first time in many years split their endorsement. My former Deputy Secretary of State, William Hettiger, enjoyed most of the labor support several weeks prior to the state convention. However, the UAW suddenly decided against Hettiger and, prior to the state convention, caucused with their leadership at UAW headquarters deciding to support James McNeely. This endorsement by the UAW lead to a split in the labor ranks with the AFL-CIO unions supporting Hettiger and the UAW supporting McNeely.

On the day of the convention in Detroit it was a toss up as to who would be elected. The selection of a new state chairman was even more complicated with Otto Feinstein's entrance into the race. He had the support of the ultra-liberal New Democratic Coalition group and the candidacy of Bernie Klein, the Comptroller of the City of Detroit and Mayor Cavanaugh's candidate for chairman. It appeared that the candidacies of Feinstein and Klein were taking votes away from Hettiger and McNeely and, as a matter of fact, representatives of these two candidates approached Hettiger to form a coalition to defeat the UAW candidate, McNeely. Their proposal was rejected by Hettiger. On the day of the convention, the UAW felt so strongly about their endorsement of McNeely that their staff members were suggesting to the delegates that unless they supported McNeely they could not look forward to the UAW endorsement in future local and state elections. The obvious happened, McNeely was elected state chairman.

Republican William Milliken did not allow Hettiger's defeat as a candidate for Democratic state chairman to bother him. In January, 1971, when he was looking for a Director of the Department of Administration, he chose Hettiger. Milliken and Hettiger had known each other for twenty years having worked together on the Grand Traverse County Board of Supervisors. The Department of Administration has the duty by law of "securing greater administrative efficiency and economy, minimizing duplication of activities and affecting better organization and consolidation of functions among state agencies." In other words, economy and efficiency.

One of the brightest stars in labor's crown was a fight led by Gus Scholle, President of the AFL-CIO, to bring about reapportionment of the Michigan Legislature. His battle began in 1959. Previous to that time, there had been a malapportionment of legislative districts but it was becoming increasingly apparent in the Senate. Some Senate districts were four times as large in population as others but each Senator had one vote in the Michigan Legislature. The inequity of the situation was obvious. In 1959, Scholle filed a suit in the Michigan Supreme Court claiming that his rights as a voter in Oakland County were diminished by his district's proportionate lack of voice in the Senate, that these districts were arbitrary and unrepresentative, and the discrimination against him violated the "equal protection of the laws" clause of the Fourteenth Amendment. The Michigan Supreme Court dismissed the case on the grounds that the court lacked jurisdiction.

However, in March of 1962, the U.S. Supreme Court handed down the Baker vs. Carr decision thus declaring, for the first time, that the courts could scrutinize legislative apportionment for adherence to the Fourteenth Amendment's "equal protection of the laws" clause, and that continuing failure to redistrict legislatures in line with population changes would be cause for court review.*

Scholle's suit which had been appealed to the U.S. Supreme Court was remanded to the Supreme Court of Michigan for a new look in harmony with the Baker doctrine. In July of 1962, the Michigan Supreme Court reversed its earlier decision, citing Baker, and declared that Michigan's 1952 apportionment was illegal. However, in April of 1963, voters approved a new constitution which included, among its provisions, that the apportionment of the state senate should be with consideration of both population and area in laying out new senate geographic districts. Scholle countered this by bringing a new court test, this time in the Federal District Court, in case the first suit was moot. He again charged that the senate provisions of the new constitution also violated his rights as a voter under the Fourteenth Amendment.*

In September of 1963, the Apportionment Commission established by the new constitution began its deliberations in order to reconcile the eighty/twenty formula, which considered both population and area, with the implications of the Baker vs. Carr decision. This Commission, with four Democrats and four Republicans, chosen by their respective parties from four broad districts in the state, could not agree on any plan. The Republicans stood behind the population-area concept, and Democrats insisted on a one-man one-vote or equal population districts. The constitution provided that in the event of a deadlock by the Apportionment Commission, the Michigan Supreme Court would choose the plan which best complied with the constitution. Before this choice could be made by the court, another landmark decision came from Washington. In June, 1964, the U.S. Supreme Court declared, in the Reynolds vs. Sims case, that both houses of the state legislature should be based on a standard of population in order to satisfy the Fourteenth Amendment. In keeping with this ruling, the

*Carolyn Stieber: *The Politics of Change in Michigan* (Michigan State University Press, 1970).

Michigan Supreme Court had to choose the Democratic plan, called the Austin-Kleiner Plan, which redistricted both Michigan legislative houses entirely on a population basis.* In the end, it was a great personal triumph for Gus Scholle, and certainly a feather in labor's cap.

I was not a disinterested spectator while this was going on. First, as the chief election officer of Michigan, I was the defendant of all the Gus Scholle suits. Never was a defendant more in the position of trying to lose his case. In addition, by law, I was the official Secretary of the Reapportionment Commission for the many months that it met, and at that time I observed the fine work done by one of the Democratic members of the Apportionment Commission, Richard Austin, whom I later supported in his campaign for Secretary of State.

You will note that up to this point I have had almost nothing to say about the Teamsters Union, yet it is one of the most powerful unions in the country. The reason for my lack of comment is that I have had almost no contact with the Teamsters Union in campaigns or elections, with one *possible* exception. In mid-summer of 1960, when I was campaigning for the nomination for the gubernatorial race, I received a phone call from a friend who was an official with one of the race tracks in the state. He arranged for us to meet, confidentially, at a restaurant outside of Detroit. His proposition was an interesting one. He said he had some friends who would be interested in financially supporting me in my campaign for the Democratic gubernatorial nomination. They were prepared to give me almost any sum I deemed necessary to win that race. He went on to say that his friends were not so enamored with me, but were in opposition to my opponent in that race for the nomination. He said, "He is the UAW's boy and we would like to have a boy of our own." I explained my opposition to spending large amounts of money for political campaigns and declined his offer with thanks. That terminated the interview and no further contacts were made. You can draw your own conclusion as to whether I have ever had contact with the Teamsters Union or not.

* *Ibid.* pp.36–37.

III

THE LEGAL FRATERNITY

IN a previous chapter I pointed out that the labor movement, and particularly the UAW, was a potent force in the Democratic Party. Now I must point out the group which is the most dominant and the most effective force in state government, regardless of the political party involved. That is the legal fraternity. My father, who was an attorney, used to tell me of the glories of the profession and the values of the adversary procedure which, he declared, guaranteed that justice would be rendered in the American courts. To put it mildly, I have gathered some doubts since that time. I did put my father's certificate on the wall of my office, since his name and mine were exactly the same, and unless you examined the graduation date of 1894, from the Detroit College of Law, I could pontificate to the less knowledgeable about legal complexities.

My legal education began immediately after I entered office in 1955. At that time I paid a visit to the Director of the Civil Service Commission, Arthur Rasch, to discuss the hiring of attorneys by my office. Rasch poured cold water on my ideas and said that I would have to use the office of the Attorney General for my legal services. I could hire attorneys so long as I did not allow them to practice in court or so long as they had no real legal duties. This I did and these persons were titled Administrative Aides. (One aide, Milo Chalfant, became a nationally known consultant on motor vehicle codes.) Unfortunately, after they had worked on any particular case or drafted bills for the Legislature, they had to drop the matter at hand and then the assigned Assistant Attorney General was called in. When Rasch was explaining to me my relationship to the legal profession, he assured me with a wry grin and chuckle that some people felt that having to use an attorney from another office was something like attempting to get a divorce from your wife while she hired and paid your attorney. I cannot really fault any Assistant Attorney General, but must point out that this system simply takes the natural course of having any Assistant Attorney General more loyal to the Attorney General who appoints, promotes and pays him, than to a department head upon whom he has no dependence economically.

It was not long before I understood why Rasch had both grinned and chuckled when he assured me that the relationship between the Attorney General lawyers and myself would not be that of an ordinary attorney and his client. In 1956, the branch manager who sold license plates in St. Clair Shores took off for Mexico with her husband and with $80,000 of the state's money. I was not unduly concerned because I knew that the Secretary of State's office was bonded and the bonding company involved promptly paid out the full bond on the branch manager involved. This happened to be $50,000, which left another $30,000 to be recovered. The state then took over the home and car of the manager and certain small amounts of money that she had left in the bank. But, after recovering all possible money from these sources, there still was a discrepancy of $13,000.

The agent for the bonding company then came in to talk with me and told me that his company would, of course, be willing to pay off that $13,000 to the state on *my* bond, but that as soon as they did so they would hold me responsible and sue to recover that money from me personally. To put it mildly, this was a shock. I went to the Attorney General, Thomas Kavanaugh, to seek what legal advice I could in the situation and received another shock. He said that it was with great regret that he had to tell me that his first duty was to the state and not to protect my personal interest—I was on my own and maybe I should go out and hire an attorney. My friends thought this was a hilarious situation. They painted vivid pictures of my car being confiscated, my house taken and me thrown into debtors prison. Carl

Rudow of the *Detroit News* wrote a kind of gag story on the situation, which was all sympathy but no money. As a result of that story one good citizen, whom I remember warmly, sent me a check for ten dollars to apply against ths $13,000. Meanwhile, I was in need of an attorney and as a result of the *Detroit News* story the firm of Butzel, Levin, Winston and Quint volunteered to counsel and advise me. Their interest in the case was spurred on by one of the lawyers in the firm, a personal friend of mine, Patrick J. Foley. After a month, they gave me their advice: I did not have a prayer. Once I accepted the $13,000 from the bonding company, that company had every legal right to step in and take over whatever assets I had to recover the $13,000.

Another newspaper story resulted from this and the publicity brought a special bonus. Senator Elmer Porter, the Republican from Blissfield, and Chairman of the Senate Finance Committee, walked into my office, needled me a bit, and then said, "we'll take care of the situation, don't worry about it." He was as good as his word and a resolution was drafted and passed by the Senate that took me off the hook for the $13,000.

The Attorney General was perfectly right, he had to defend the position of the state first, but it certainly was no help to me as an individual in an untenable situation. My Deputy at that time, Billie Farnum, said the situation was not all bad because he and Attorney General Kavanaugh took a plane trip to Mexico City to look for the culprits. They never found them because they were in a town on the west coast of Mexico, five hundred miles away. Later on they were apprehended, brought back to Michigan and sentenced to prison.

This was my first lesson in the complexities of law. I was to get another at the very end of my last term which was slightly different but still involved the question of having an attorney working for one who was hired and paid by another office. This concerned the anti-parochiaid petitions gathered by the Council Against Parochiaid (CAP). They had been able to collect, in the summer and fall of 1970, some 320,000 signatures seeking a state wide vote on a constitutional amendment prohibiting public aid to non-public schools. During the period that the petitions were being circulated, Attorney General Kelley had given an opinion that the petitions were invalid and the format of the petitions insufficient to meet the constitutional requirements for amending the 1963 constitution. Consequently, the State Board of Canvassers refused to certify the petitions filed by CAP and that organization then filed suit in the Court of Appeals seeking a *mandamus* action against the Secretary of State forcing him to canvass the petitions and put the proposed amendment on the state-wide ballot. The Appeals Court ordered the official canvass to be filed with their court on September 2. Then the Michigan Court of Appeals ruled by two to one that the parochiaid petitions were valid. This overruled the Attorney General's opinion, and the Court gave permission for the amendment to appear on the November 3 ballot.

The Attorney General responded immediately to the Court's action. I read in the newspapers that Kelley had filed an "Emergency Application for Leave to Appeal to the Supreme Court." This disturbed me first of all because I wanted to see the proposed amendment on the November 3 ballot so that the people could make a decision and, secondly and even more pertinent to our office, was the fact that I knew if the legal questions became snarled up in the Supreme Court it might take days or weeks to get a decision. I was very fearful that the Supreme Court might hand down a decision in very late October or even the first day of November and order that the amendment go on the November 3 ballot. This, of course, would be an impossible situation for the county clerks who needed lead time of several weeks to have the ballots printed. They were already calling the office of the Director of Elections, and asking what could be done to prevent such a thing happening.

When I received a copy of the official "Leave to Appeal to the Supreme Court," I was shocked to find out that the Attorney General was not appealing on his own but that I was a plaintiff in the case and a plaintiff without being consulted by the Attorney General's office. Upon discovering this, I immediately proceeded to the Attorney General's office and Leon Cohan, the Deputy Attorney General, expressed sympathy but said it had gone too far and nothing could be done to remove my name as plaintiff. With no hope of disengaging myself from the case in the Attorney General's office, I turned to the Supreme Court and, on September 8, explained the situation to Chief Justice Brennen. I asked him to use his good office to get my name off the appeal. After he had a very hearty laugh at my predicament, he said "you're in the hands of your lawyer. You better go back and see him again." It was then that the cold truth dawned on me. I found out the client was working for the attorney and not in the way it had originally been explained to me sixteen years earlier by the Director of Civil Service.

As it turned out, the Supreme Court turned down the Attorney General's appeal and in so doing upheld the Court of Appeals. The State Board of Canvassers certified the petitions, the amendment appeared on the ballot and the voters defeated parochiaid.

I was not the only department head unhappy with the lack of control over the attorneys. John Mackie, who was the Highway Commissioner from 1957 to 1964, was engaged in a very ambitious highway building program in cooperation with the federal government. In the course of building roads it was necessary to buy thousands of acres of land. Some of that land was simply bought from the owner at the price offered by the Highway Department. But other sections had to be condemned through the courts. Mackie, of course, wanted to proceed at full speed, and felt he could not do so unless he could have the scheduling of the Assistant Attorney Generals assigned to his department so that he could move them from court to court and county to county as need dictated. Mackie pointed out quite clearly that even though he owned five miles of land, if there were four hundred feet in the middle of it that the Highway Department did not own, road building in that particular township was delayed. However, Paul Adams, the Attorney General (1958–61) who had succeeded Kavanaugh, was in no mood to release his control over the Assistant Attorney Generals. It was finally resolved by the appointment of special Assistant Attorney Generals, who were in the general law practice in various parts of the state. These lawyers were able to move in, under the direction of the Attorney General, on the local level and get the job of condemning the necessary lands done.

Mackie also had another experience with the Attorney General's office, which for him was even worse. He had left office as Highway Commissioner at the end of 1964. However, in 1965, 1966 and 1967 allegations and accusations began to flow about the Capitol that, during his administration, some of the highway contractors were improperly paid for their services, and that substantial sums had been paid out to them without statutory authority. Furthermore, rumor had it that these same favored highway contractors paid kickbacks into certain unspecified political funds. Attorney General Kelley began a formal investigation of these allegations after some prodding by Governor Romney. The investigation, which took some months, was done by members of the Attorney General's staff, and, indeed, in some cases by the same members who had worked as legal counsel for the State Highway Department during Mackie's term of office. In other words, the lawyers who had put their imprimatur of approval on certain contracts with highway builders were now the inquisitors and investigators for the Attorney General's office.

It was not difficult for these Assistant Attorney Generals to legally switch hats. They had every legal justification to be, at one point, legal counsel for the Highway Department and two or three years later to become investigators for the Attorney General's staff. But for the man being investigated, John Mackie, it could well be a nightmare, since he was of the opinion that the transactions being questioned in 1967 had been approved by the very persons who were now investigating those transactions. Yet Mackie had to accept the onus of any misfeasance or malfeasance involved. Personally, I always suspected that there was a slight conflict of interest on the part of the Assistant Attorney Generals in the investigation. The net result of the Attorney General's final report, in July of 1967, was to commence a Grand Jury. Nonetheless, the practice of having one department control the legal staff for another department seemed to me to be manifestly unfair. In the end, which was 1969, the Grand Jury exonerated Mackie of all wrongdoing and did not indict a single highway contractor.

I always thought it would have been poetic justice if all the secretaries used by the attorneys in the Attorney General's office had been hired, promoted, and paid by the Secretary of State's office. It would have been very comparable to this situation of the Attorney General controlling the legal talent used by all other departments of state government. But I am sure there would have been a terrible furor from the legal group, had any such organizational change been proposed.

One of the difficulties of a department head in this system is that he is dependent upon an Attorney General who may remove himself from office by running for another office or being defeated. In that case, of course, a new Attorney General is either elected or appointed by the Governor. Attorney Generals, like all other attorneys I know, think rather independently. Theoretically, at least, they only interpret the law and do not make it. However the interpretation of Attorney Generals or Supreme Court Judges is extremely flexible. I need not point out that even in the U.S. Supreme Court there may be seven men looking at the same law and the same facts and come up with widely different opinions, so it is most important to a department head that he have some continuity as to how the law will be interpreted and how the opinions from the Attorney General's office will read.

One may say yes, it is probably not an ideal situation but since all the departments have to conform to it, it cannot be too bad. That is the rub. The requirement that the Attorney General's office be used for legal services does not apply across the board. The Governor's office selects and hires and pays his own legal counsel. The Civil Service Commission does likewise, as do the universities. Since many of the questions asked by executive department heads have political tinges to them, it would be absurd for example to have a Republican Governor completely dependent upon a Democratic Attorney General for his legal advice or counterwise. That, of course, has happened in Michigan on several occasions within the last two decades. However, the two offices of state government who have been most strongly supportive of the Attorney General in his demand to control all legal talent are the Governor's office and the Civil Service Commission. It is a case of do as I say and not as I do.

Some seven years ago the Civil Service Commission decided that they would force the Secretary of State's office to put all license plate branch managers under the Civil Service, rather than have them appointed by the Secretary of State himself. This case has been meandering through the courts ever since. It has been in the Appellate Court, Circuit Court and the State Supreme Court, and I think is now back in the Ingham County Circuit Court.* But the interesting thing about this case is that if the Attorney General changed, it could well mean a change in the official legal position of the state which presently is that the Civil Service Commission does not have the right to force the Secretary of State to hire only Civil Service employees. The Attorney General, beyond the question of the law itself, has a personal interest in this because if the precedent be set that a department head had to have Civil Service employees, this would vastly restrict his ability to choose private attorneys for his own department.

On the other hand, the Civil Service Commission was in a most peculiar position. They had always advocated that departments should use attorneys only from the Attorney General's office and that those attorneys should be civil servants. Now the Commission was in a bind because they wanted no part of the Attorney General's advice or help, and so they went out on the open market and hired their own attorney, a non-civil servant to represent them in the court case. This was to me, of course, a most interesting development because they were going entirely contrary to the regulations they laid down for me to operate with. I must admit it was the only direction they could go, pragmatically it was most justifiable. But what is justifiable for one

*This case was terminated August 1971, by a consent judgement between the Secretary of State and the Civil Service Commission. It was agreed that the fee branch offices would be transferred to classified Civil Service offices at a rate of not less than fifteen per cent of the business volume per year.

department head should be justifiable for another.

The defense that I tried to raise in this case was that a patronage system in this particular instance was a much more economical one to operate, and was statistically very easy to prove since a branch office system under patronage would cost about two million dollars, while a Civil Service system would cost at least four million dollars to operate. Two different systems were involved, one in which you were paying people only for service rendered, selling license plates, transferring titles etc., while in a Civil Service situation, you were paying people by the hour and if there was no business due to weather or seasonable ups and downs, they continued to be paid whether much went on in that office or not.

The two hundred or more branch managers that I had appointed were noticeably upset during the first two years that the case was fought out in the courts. They felt that they never knew when the axe would fall. I met with them in groups around the state fairly regularly and tried to keep them up-to-date as to what the legal situation was, but I was forced to rely only on oral explanations I had been given by the Attorney General's office since, in spite of the fact the case had lasted many years, I never had a written memo on the case from the Attorney General's office. This upset the branch managers even more.

At this point, Attorney General Frank Kelley indicated he might be interested in running for another office, and it was conceivable that he might win that office. If a Republican Governor was in office at that moment he, of course, would replace Kelley with a Republican choice. All of these facts convinced the branch managers group to hire their own private attorney to defend their interests in holding their jobs, which were somewhat different from my interest in retaining the fee-system, patronage-control branch office organization. When the branch managers took this step, we had a situation in which there was one law firm defending their interest and the Attorney General's office defending my interest, but once again demonstrating the difficulties of having an Attorney General act as legal counsel for other departments.

Not all the troubles were between the Attorney General's office and the department heads. There were also problems between governmental department heads and the judiciary. One interesting case that is unforgettable to me came on December 19, 1968, when I read in the newspapers that a driver, whom I shall call FM, was still driving a car with a perfectly valid drivers license about eleven weeks after he admitted in court that he had killed a man and his wife, and had been convicted of negligent homicide. The penalty for this conviction is a mandatory one and the State Department is required to revoke the license of the person involved. The first stories printed suggested that I had been negligent in my duty. But an investigation into the record of the particular driver quickly showed that the court that had convicted him had never sent us an abstract of conviction, and, therefore, it had never been put on his record in our computer. This was an old story to me, the fact that the courts, when they convict a man of traffic violations, do not always comply with the law by sending in that abstract of conviction. The vehicle code required it be sent in within ten days of the date of the conviction but there are innumerable cases in which there may be a delay of some three months to a year before that conviction abstract reaches the office. This, of course, causes immeasureable trouble for the police officer on patrol duty because he may stop a motorist, radio in to our computer to get his record, and not know that the record is in error because it is incomplete.

I wrestled with this delinquency of the courts for over ten years. I even tried calling some of the judges who were particularly late in getting their reports in. Some of them accepted my call in good grace and perhaps improved their procedures, but others told me very frankly that I was a part of the executive office of government and could not coerce the judges in any way. They were right. I could not and I did not, but I did take my plea and complaint to the Supreme Court by way of asking the Court Administrator, Bill Hart, a long time friend, to ask the members of the Supreme Court to look over the situation and try to give us some help, since the Supreme Court has supervising control over the other courts. He explained that many judges are very touchy on this subject of being coerced or ordered by their judicial superiors but that he would pass the message along to the other members. I do know that they talked about it, but I must admit that I did not see, by the end of my term of office, any great improvement in the promptness of conviction abstracts coming in.

In 1967 another controversy broke out between state agencies and the State Bar Association. Burke Dailey, Director of the Workmen's Compensation Bureau, made complaints about lawyers' misconduct and referred about one hundred of these complaints to the State Bar for action. By October of 1968, Dailey made public complaint that "it appears to us that the State Bar is unwilling and unable to handle the task of stopping these illegal practices." Finally, on October 30, 1969, the *Detroit Free Press* editorialized on the situation and I fear it reflected the general public's viewpoint. Their editorial stated, in part:

The Whitewash which A.D. Ruegsegger, president of the State Bar of Michigan, tried to splash over his union Tuesday wasn't thick enough.

The ugly areas—such as the 'claims mills' in the workmen's compensation field, the grievance procedures and the new rules of conduct—still show through.

Mr. Ruegsegger, a Detroiter, was trying to answer the charges made by Burke Dailey director of the Workmen's Compensation Bureau, that the bureau has referred more than 100 compaints of lawyer misconduct to the state Bar for action since 1967 and the State Bar has done little about them.

Mr. Dailey said his department will seek legal authority to purge offending attorneys from appearing before it because: 'It appears to us that the State Bar of Michigan is unwilling and unable to handle the task of stopping these illegal practices.'

Mr. Ruegsegger replied the Dailey charges were 'without good foundation,' and that the bar 'does not intend to tolerate and condone any unethical or illegal practices.'

If this were the first such instance, we might give Mr. Ruegsegger the benefit of the doubt. But it isn't.

The State Bar has habitually and callously ignored or stalled complaints. It has taken little significant action to clean itself up. And the only time it has acted against mis-mal- or non-feasance on the part of lawyers has been after diligent public prodding and under the bright glare of publicity.

In a speech he gave at the American Bar Association convention in August, Mr. Ruegsegger said that the State Bar 'had been working on these (workmen's compensation) cases for a lengthy period of time in co-operation with the state police and the Michigan Workmen's Compensation Department.'

Yet, as Mr. Dailey said, only one attorney has been punished, and in that case he voluntarily surrendered his license.

. . . . .

Not all lawyers, as individuals, are guilty, of course, but in Michigan all lawyers belong to the State Bar and the State Bar is guilty.

And it is small wonder that even Mr. Ruegsegger, apologist plenipotentiary for the State Bar, felt called upon to quote, in his August speech, from Carl Sandburg:

'Why is there always a secret singing
When a lawyer cashes in?
Why does a hearse horse snicker
Hauling a lawyer away?'

Do not believe that all the controversy between governmental agencies and the bar associations takes place in Michigan. The very outspoken mayor of Salt Lake City had this to say in a news article in the *Salt Lake Tribune* of October 26, 1970.

Salt Lake City Mayor J. Bracken Lee said Tuesday he was quoted correctly in the Salt LakeTribune in saying: 'The law profession is a special group. You have a license to steal and we dont.'

J. Thomas Greene, president of the Utah State Bar, wrote the mayor on August 19 and said the 'matter of that quotation came before the board of bar commissioners of the Utah State Bar and the commissioners would like to know whether the quotation correctly sets forth what you stated. Perhaps you were misquoted in some respect.'

'For you information, I was quoted correctly' Mayor Lee replied. 'That statement was made directly to an attorney in a commission meeting July 30, 1970, and indicates my true feelings concerning your profession.'

I do not contend, however, that all lawyers have availed

themselves of this license, but I still insist they are privileged to commit certain violations of the law with impunity. I would like to point out the distinction that exists among elective public officials. Those who belong to the law profession are never prosecuted for taking retainers or fees for services rendered which in many instances would be considered bribery or graft if accepted by a public official who is not a member of your profession.

But enough of the in-fighting between government officials and the Bar Association. What does the general public think of the legal profession? I learned, somewhat to my shock and sorrow, during the past four years from what I shall call the "Turner Episode" in Livingston County. James Turner, from Howell, Michigan, was a businessman who published a small weekly newspaper in that town. Some years ago he became interested in some probate court practices in which the beneficiaries of certain estates had not received their due from those estates over a long period of time. As he proceeded with his investigation he became more and more convinced that the whole legal apparatus in that county was working together, not in the interest of their clients, but in the financial interest of the attorneys themselves. Turner, as a result of these investigations, became very active politically on the county level. He stirred up the citizenry to an unbelievable degree and in the elections of November 1969, Turner's slate took over the offices of Circuit Judge, Prosecuter, Attorney, Sheriff and County Clerk. The interesting thing about that entire campaign was that it was based on a condemnation of the legal profession in Livingston County and the vested interests of the county never had a chance. The general public agreed strongly with the position that Turner took.

Meanwhile, Turner started a magazine which was published throughout the State of Michigan and which also attacked what he termed to be the corruption of the legal profession in many communities and counties throughout the state. However, Turner's life was far from simple. His forceful and outspoken personality often got him in trouble. On one particular case he was cited for contempt of court and sentenced by the late Judge Breakey of Ann Arbor to fifteen days in jail. Turner appealed this to the Michigan Court of Appeals and almost two years later, by unanimous opinion, they did clear him of the contempt charge. A *Free Press* editorial of December 12, 1969, comments on the situation:

> The Second division of the Michigan Court of Appeals added little luster to the judicial profession with its unanimous opinion clearing James C. Turner of contempt of court.
>
> The judges made the right decision for the weakest possible reasons. They relied entirely on federal law and U.S. Supreme Court decisions which were already in existence when Turner was originally convicted of contempt. They issued no warnings to lower courts to prevent future repetitions.
>
> And of possibly even greater significance, they allowed a naive reader to infer from their decision that all is right and beautiful with the administration of justice as practiced by Judge Michael J. Carland who, at the time of the supposed contempt, was the circuit judge of Livingston and Shiawassee counties, now only of the latter.
>
> Mr. Turner got in trouble with the law when, nearly two years ago, he charged that a Livingston County lawyer, Martin J. Lavan, who has since been barred from the practice of law, 'has almost totally corrupted the entire judicial system' in the county and that 'the judge and most of the attorneys either live in fear of this man, or, for some reason, are afraid or won't speak out against the system.'
>
> This hit Judge Carland where he lived. Not only was he the circuit judge, but he was an old-time buddy of Lavan's. So he promptly ordered Turner to show cause why he should not be judged in contempt of court.
>
> The fact that decision after decision in the Supreme Court limited contempt convictions to incidents in which the actual administration of justice was 'immediately imperiled' was of no concern to Judge Carland. Nor was it any concern of the late Judge James Breakey of Ann Arbor who heard the contempt case, found Turner guilty, fined him $150 and sentenced him to 15 days in jail.
>
> Judge Breakey wasn't even impressed by the ancient concept of presumed innocence. Rather than order Judge Carland to

show why Turner was guilty, he ordered Turner to prove his innocence.

This was in June of last year, and it is a commentary of the operation of the court that only now has the Court of Appeals handed down a decision in so transparent a case.

Transparent, we say, because all the precedents already on the books were duly cited by the Court of Appeals. The judges ticked them off with singular stolidity. They turned down Judge Carland's argument that Turner's charges 'poisoned' public opinion about the court.

And there's the rub. In turning down the argument, the Court of Appeals sought to create the impression that Judge Carland was a study of rectitude. It didn't say that, but a casual reader might draw that conclusion.

We cannot accept the mistaken syllogism that allegations of corruption in and of themselves create corruption. Petitioner (Carland) needs no defense of his position other than an impeccable reputation as a jurist.

Then, later on, the court said, 'The Livingston bench was made the subject of disparaging statements. The best defense they may present to the public is the unsullied performance of their judicial duties.'

Again, the court didn't say the Livingston bench was unsullied, but again the invitation is offered to take it that way.

It isn't that way at all, as a leisurely and incomplete investigation by the State Bar of Michigan has shown.

In its decision, the Court of Appeals offered Judge Carland two courses of action. One is a public record of unsullied performance. If he can't provide that, he can sue for libel. Judge Carland has filed no such suit.

But what he can't do is hide behind his judicial robes. As the court said, quoting Justice Hugo Black, 'The assumption that respect for the judiciary can be won by shielding judges from published criticism wrongly appraises the character of American public opinion.'

In the winter of 1969, I attended a meeting in Owosso, Michigan, called by Turner to talk about the legal situation in Shiawassee County. That meeting, held in zero weather, was attended by thirteen hundred people in the armory of that town, with another two hundred standing outside listening to loud speakers. The talk that Turner gave was a diatribe against the officials of the county and the legal profession in general. The shocking thing about it to me was the absolute acceptance of the audience of what he had to say, and their derisive comments on the legal profession. It was driven home to me that a great sector of the Michigan public hold the legal profession in contempt, suspicion and distrust.

Such a malevolent opinion of the profession by the public is intolerable. If it persists, this state and this country are in serious trouble. Certainly the legal codes, the courts, and the lawyers themselves have for generations been absolute pillars in our society. To have that pillar shattered means that our culture is also in serious trouble. Turner continued his attacks on the profession and struck out in all directions. No court was safe from his attack. I was criticized in an article he wrote in one of his magazines, but on the whole I thought that Turner's criticisms had substantial merit since they showed at least one person was looking into the dark spots of public life and bringing them to light.

Finally, Turner ran for Governor in the election of 1970, and was, as expected, defeated in the primary by another Republican, the incumbent William Milliken. However, Turner's campaign again depended on his criticism of the legal profession, and I thought he made a very creditable run since he had almost no money to work with, and his name was largely unknown throughout the state. I would predict that he will be heard from in the future and that hopefully some of his attacks and recommendations will bear fruit.

What brought about this distaste on the part of the public for the legal profession? Certainly it did not exist twenty years ago as it does today. The comments of the man in the street are revealing. He thinks that the profession demands and gets special privileges; that attorneys are amoral in being able to take any side of a controversy for a fee; that they exist as a tight union which protects its own members, and, as one man said to me, "they cover for each other as though they were a legal mafia." In addition, the public is aware that the profession controls its own destiny. To be a judge you must be a lawyer, and decisions in the lower courts must be authenticated by other lawyers in the Appellate Court and the Supreme Court. The Prosecuting Attorneys and the Attorney General are lawyers and in the legislative chambers the judiciary committees are completely owned by other lawyers. No change could ever be made in a law affecting them without their full consent. This last point, of course, is all important because if reforms in the legal structure and the judiciary are to be made, they are going to have to go through the judiciary committees of the House and Senate. I think the public also holds the profession guilty of making judicial procedures so slow that literally thousands of persons are held in the jails of this state awaiting trial. They are held responsible for the slowness and logjams in the courts. As one man said, "I don't think they want change. The logjams in the courts keep a lawyer in business for a long time before a settlement is reached." Certainly he was right in assigning the responsibility for changing the judicial system. If anyone is going to do it, it would have to be the legal profession.

What is the answer? There are certain possible goals. First, the profession needs supervision, and someone from the general public looking over its shoulder to a greater degree. I believe that the legal profession should be licensed by a state agency rather than by their own Bar Association. No other occupation or profession operating in Michigan is self-licensing and self-policing. If the doctors, architects, plumbers and cosmetologists can be licensed by a state agency, certainly the legal profession could also. Probably a worse fault which needs correcting is the self-policing powers of the law group. It is too much to ask that any group of attorneys sit on a board and listen to grievances about other members of their profession, when that grievance board was chosen by the very persons and the very group being investigated.

The situation became so bad that early in 1970 the Supreme Court took official notice. On January 8, 1970, the Gongwer News Service, under the headline "Supreme Court Creates Legal Watchdog Panel" reported the action of the Supreme Court.

The Supreme Court today announced creation of a special grievance board empowered to police the conduct of the State's 11,000 lawyers and disbar those found in violation of a strict new code of conduct.

The new State Bar Grievance Board will assume the function of the State Bar, which has been under fire for alleged failure to crack-down on errant lawyers.

While acknowledging those complaints about the Bar's enforcement activities, Chief Justice Thomas E. Brennan emphasized that the commissioners of the Bar had worked closely with the court in establishing the new policing board and other recent rule changes to curb misconduct by Bar members.

Three of the five lawyers to serve on the board will be appointed by the Bar Commissioners. The Supreme Court will name two more, as well as two laymen. Michigan's board will be 'perhaps unique' in the Nation by inclusion of non-lawyers, Mr. Brennan said.

Creation of the board, whose members will officially take office on March 1, is authorized in a new Supreme Court rule (no. 15). The rule states that the board will 'constitute the arm of the Supreme Court for the discharge of its exclusive constitutional responsibility to supervise and discipline the members of the State Bar of Michigan.'

The new rule also authorizes the board to appoint a grievance administrator and a staff of investigators to check complaints regarding lawyers' conduct. Creation of hearing panels, each comprising three lawyers, is also authorized.

The final order of the grievance board is appealable only to the Supreme Court itself.

The cost of the board and its agents is to be borne by the Bar.

The Supreme Court also revised Rule 14, which provides standards of conduct for lawyers.

The new system has been effect for over a year, and is apparently improving the situation. However, I shall reserve judgment on whether this new watchdog board will function any better than the one that was a part of the Michigan Bar Association. My qualms and doubts are because the composition of the new board will still have five attorneys out of seven, and the expenses of the new board will be paid by the Michigan Bar Association.

Finally, the question is whether the judges, prosecuting attorneys and members of the judiciary committees of the Legislature will put the general welfare of the state ahead of the personal needs of the profession. Certainly if the reputation of the profession is not redeemed soon, we are in sad shape. The experience of State Representative Thomas Sharpe, who introduced a bill to have the state license attorneys rather than having it done in private by the Bar Association, is revealing. That bill, introduced with considerable courage, died aborning in the judiciary committee of the Legislature—as could have been expected.

The Supreme Court, in January of 1970, reinforced the public image of the legal profession as one of special privilege and interests. At that time the seven judges of the Supreme Court unanimously struck down an Administrative Order requiring them to pay fifty cents a day to park their state-owned cars in the Capitol complex underground garages. They took this action in an official order to insure that "the judicial process may continue to function without interruption, uncertainty or confusion." They won no friends among the state workers by this action, since all other state employees continued to pay the fifty cent fee. The judges, of course, won the battle, and no longer paid the fee. However, they could have made their legal point very well and voluntarily agreed to pay the fifty cent fee.

The Michigan Bar Association is beginning to show some awareness of their public image and is attempting to make some corrections. In February of 1969, the Bar Association President, Gilbert Davis, in the association's monthly journal, stated that Michigan lawyers had been warned that unless they improved the policing of the law profession, it would surely undergo radical and dramatic changes in Michigan. In 1971, Chief Justice Kavanaugh, of the Supreme Court, challenged the Legislature to provide the Michigan Supreme Court with money and manpower to streamline the state's judicial process, especially in Detroit. He outlined programs costing more than two million dollars and asked the Legislature to authorize twenty three additional judgeships, nineteen of them in Detroit. He recommended a system of compulsory and accelerated pre-trial procedures which hopefully could cut the delays now evident from the present fifteen months to a manageable period of time.

From my criticism of the legal profession, it may appear that I have a personal animosity against lawyers. This is not true. I have received aid and free counsel from an innumerable group of attorneys throughout the state. However, I am convinced that the organization of the legal profession in this state is entirely wrong since it destroys the most important thing it needs: public confidence and approbation. I shudder to think what would happen if this deterioration of reputation accelerates. At best, the young people are suspicious of the establishment, and the worse thing that could happen would be to find that their suspicions were correct and that the profession, or individuals in it, were not living up to their ethics and canons, and that nothing was being done about it.

I have always found it very strange that the young liberal lawyers who were in the forefront of demanding reform and equal rights all over the country never turned their efforts toward their own profession.

IV

THE GRAND JURY
vs THE OMBUDSMAN

THE one-man grand jury in Michigan is an interesting organism. It has performed yeoman service over the years. One grand jury resulted in the conviction of top officials in both Detroit and Wayne County, and another dealing with members of the state Legislature brought to light many unsavory things. The official prosecutors of the persons indicted by certain grand juries have had meteoric careers in politics later on. One became a governor, another a U.S. senator, so there are great political implications whenever a grand jury is called. Simply stated, a grand jury is designated to ascertain whether the evidence of alleged violations on the part of public officials is sufficient to warrant trial by a lesser court. The grand jury does not pass judgment or convict any of the persons involved, but only indicts them and recommends them for further trial.

The powers of a grand jury are great and the greatest is the right to subpoena reluctant witnesses. In this way, a grand jury differs from the powers of the state's Attorney General who does not have the right to subpoena a witness, and thereby is hindered in the prosecution of any investigation. It also has some defects, one of which is that persons who are called before a grand jury to testify very often find their reputation is impugned simply by reason of their appearance. Unfortunately all grand juries tend to be in the public eye so that even though the grand juror attempts to protect the innocent witness, reporters often surround his courtroom and interrogate any person who appears. A second drawback to the grand jury system is the difficulty of getting it underway. Because it is such a powerful instrument of investigation, and hopefully of justice, it is necessary to have a strong case before a grand jury can be called. One grand jury that stands out in my mind was the one involved in the investigation of the Highway Department, in which I had only tangential involvement rather than the direct contact I desired.

The steps leading to the Highway Department grand jury were rather low key. At the State Administrative Board meetings, Governor Romney asked several questions regarding the payment of "over runs" to highway contractors. These "over runs" were sums of money paid by the state to highway contractors who alleged that they needed more money than their original bid had stated. They needed it because in the bidding process they were not warned of difficulties such as rock formations or quicksand, which raised their costs significantly. Governor Romney argued that if these "over runs" were paid without sufficient investigation it made a farce of the bidding process, in which only the contractor with the lowest bid for a stretch of road, would get the contract. The Governor requested special reports from the Highway Commission to justify the "over runs" and still was not satisfied. Finally, Romney demanded that the Attorney General make a special investigation of the situaton. During this period, many Democrats felt Governor Romney was engaging in political feuding directed against John Mackie, who had been the Highway Commissioner from 1957 through 1964. The post of Highway Commissioner had been abolished by the new constitution of 1963 and Mackie was subsequently elected Congressman from Genesee County. Thus, he was not connected with the Highway Department when these allegations were being made.

Kelley acceded to Romney's demand for a full-fledged investigation and on July 24, 1967, after several months of intensive effort, he issued a formal report. The Gongwer News Service report of that day capsules Kelley's findings.

REPORT RAPS HIGHWAY DEPARTMENT ADMINIS-
TRATION: The Highway Department granted preferential
treatment to certain contractors and paid them 'substantial
sums of money' without statutory authority, Attorney General
Frank J. Kelley charged today in a 92-page investigative report.

The Report, six months in the making, rapped two former
directors of the department for 'mismanagement' and another
top official for 'extremely poor judgment.'

'But', said Mr. Kelley, 'there is insufficient evidence to support a finding beyond a reasonable doubt that any (department)
official or employe is guilty of violating the criminal laws of this
State.'

While dismissing the need for a grand jury investigation of the
department, Mr. Kelley said he is prepared to request one if new
evidence 'demonstrates the need for such extraordinary action.'

After Kelley's report was issued, my interest in the situation heightened because monies which had been paid out to highway contractors
had first been approved by the Highway Department, then by the
highway subcommittee of the Administrative Board and finally by the
total Administrative Board, of which I was a member. My concern
was not primarily with what was going on in the Highway Department, but rather, if these allegations were true, could not the same
kind of scullduggery be going on in other departments by winning
approval through the State Administrative Board. This Board, by law,
consisted of the Governor, Lieutenant Governor, Secretary of State,
Attorney General, State Treasurer and Superintendent of Public Instruction. On August 8, the Highway Commission reacted to Kelley's
report and ordered that $800,000 be collected in over-payments to
contractors. They also presented a summary of eleven recommendations to prevent the situation from occurring again. On August 16,
1967, Prosecuting Attorney Donald Reisig of Ingham County sent a
letter to the Attorney General commenting on the possibility of a
grand jury and offering his help. In addition, he made numerous
recommendations which hopefully would prevent a situation such as
the highway affair from occurring again in state government. Copies
of this letter went to several high officials in state government. One

paragraph of this six page letter fascinated me and I quote it in its entirety.

> (3) Review should be made of all state legislation affecting public contracts and provision should be made either by new legislation or by enforceable administrative rule governing relationships between parties doing business with the state and employees, officers and agents of the state. Clearly delineated grounds should be developed for declaring contracts void and for disqualification of persons from doing future business with the state in cases of infraction thereof. This type of regulation should affect not only the Michigan State Highway Department, but all other agencies of the state. Simultaneously therewith, there should be active encouragement of the adoption by not only the road building industry, but the entire construction industry of a code of ethics governing their relationship with public entities and their employees.

The fascinating thing about this paragraph was that Reisig inferred that the same things which happened in the Highway Department could very easily be happening in the other departments of state government, and I was delighted to see this particular recommendation.

Meanwhile several things happened which influenced my thinking. On September 26, Attorney General Kelley put out a formal opinion that officials and members of boards of state colleges and universities may not serve as officials of firms doing business with the schools. He said to do so would make them guilty of a felony under the state's conflict of interest law. Dr. John Hannah, who had been one of several who asked for the opinion more than a year before, promptly resigned from the Manufacturers National Bank of Detroit and the American Bank and Trust Company of Lansing where he served as director. Two days later, the four-man State Highway Commission asked the Governor to "take necessary steps to cause a grand jury to investigate allegations of wrong doing in the state highway department prior to 1965." Since the Commission specified no investigation of action after 1964, it appeared that the effort was being made to investigate only the period when John Mackie, a Democrat, was the commissioner. Incidentally, the Highway Commission itself did not take office until November 19, 1964, therefore they would not be involved in any investigations to take place.

On September 29, Governor Romney pledged support to the State Highway Commission's request, but also limited the period to be investigated as prior to 1965. The Attorney General warned the Commission: "I will not be a party to limiting any such petition to a period only before 1965." The battle between Romney and Kelley continued for several days with Kelley expressing a viewpoint that he had insufficient evidence to bring before a grand jury. Kelley was still against limiting the period of time that a grand jury could cover in its investigation. But on October 5, both the Governor and the Attorney General suddenly muted their heated public debate and announced that they *might* make a joint petition for an investigation of the Highway Department. Kelley said he had uncovered "new information" since publishing his official report of July 24. The following day I proposed that the grand jury investigation should cover all state contracts handled by the State Administrative Board. During the next three weeks I sent four letters to Governor Romney containing evidence I thought would justify widening the grand jury investigation. I also sent copies to the Attorney General. On October 11, former Highway Commissioner John Mackie, who was now a highway consultant in Virginia after serving one term as a Congressman from the Genesee district, charged the Governor with "a deliberate attempt to impugn my integrity and professional reputation" and demanded a public apology. The day of reckoning appeared. On October 12, the Attorney General joined the Governor in requesting a grand jury investigation. Governor Romney told newsmen he agreed with the Attorney General and the investigation should be unlimited in time and should cover the administration of the department under both the State Highway Commission and under Highway Commissioner Mackie.

Unfortunately, from my viewpoint, the grand jury investigation was confined strictly to Highway Department matters and not, as I had requested, to cover all contracts made and approved by the State

Administrative Board. In other words, only one department out of nineteen in the state government would be involved in the investigation. I believed I had good reason for requesting a broadening of the investigation. Several times in the previous year and a half, certain things had happened which aroused my suspicions, but I was not in a position to sufficiently investigate nor did I have the jurisdiction or power to do so. A grand jury inquiry seemed to be the best solution. My concern stemmed from my official position as Chairman of the Building Committee of the State Administrative Board. This committee consisted of myself, as Chairman, the State Treasurer and the Attorney General. The duty of the Building Committee was to pass judgment and approve or disapprove all contracts having to do with the construction of new buildings or their repair and renovation; also the approval of leases either when the state was renting land or buildings or when private individuals were leasing from the state. Whenever a state department leased lands or buildings they would make recommendations to this committee for approval and all leases made (or so I thought) had to be approved.

As I looked back form 1967 to 1955 when I came into office, I could see that as far as the Highway Department was concerned, the State Administrative Board had approved many contracts which were now being investigated. I had approved those contracts, as had Governor Williams, Governor Romney as well as three Attorney Generals, two State Treasurers, three Superintendents of Public Instruction and two Highway Commissioners. I was pushing for the grand jury investigation at this late date, because I did not feel there was enough public knowledge that the State Administrative Board had approved those contracts. I was also much concerned that exactly the same kind of things could be going on in the Building Committee of which I was Chairman, since that committee usually accepts the recommendations of the various departments wanting new buildings or new leases.

My feelings of uneasiness stemmed from several incidents, the first of which I shall call the Tieco incident. The president of Tieco Products, Incorporated of Royal Oak, James W. Tyrer, had protested to me that his company's bid on movable petitions for the Treasury

Building had been unfairly excluded. I invited him to meet with the Building Committee and we heard his story. In essence, he had been discouraged from bidding in the beginning by the Department of Administration. Secondly, so much time had been used up before he got permission to bid, that technically his mock-up of a building petition was not submitted in time for the deadline. However, the bid he finally submitted was $55,000 lower than the next lowest bid and he made the inference that he thought the successful bidder had connections with the Department of Administration and he was being intentionally and purposely excluded by indirection. The Department of Administration denied the allegation and argued that, since the mock-up model was late in being delivered, it could not be properly evaluated and, therefore, the order for the petitions should go to the second low bidder. The Building Committee was in a quandry. The natural desire to accept the low bid from the Tieco Company and save the state $55,000 was an important consideration, but to arbitrarily order the Building Division of the Department of Administration to ignore their deadline for the evaluation of mock-ups would have contributed to organizational chaos and we would have been accused of favoritism toward a particular bidder. The upshot was that the second low bidder did get the order and the job.

Republican State Representative Tom Brown got into the act with a press release which raised numerous questions about the state's action in buying land for the capitol development complex. His most interesting statement was "what is behind the numerous allegations in the past that the state had paid greatly in excess of appraised value for land in the capitol development?" He added that he favored an extension of the grand jury investigation to look into this item. I was very much in favor of him moving into the picture.

The third incident which made me wonder what was going on was much closer to home. It concerned the lease on an office building in Lansing which the State Department shared with three other departments; Administration, Treasury and Commerce. The rent for the four tenants during the fiscal year 1965 to 1966 was just over $133,-000, with an option to renew for the same rate the following year.

Toward the end of the fiscal year, the Department of Administration informed the tenants that they had allowed their options to lapse, therefore a new lease and a new price had to be decided upon. All four tenants immediately protested that they did not negotiate the lease and only the Department of Administration had a copy of it. Thus, the tenants had not let their lease lapse intentionally. Next, the Department of Administration suggested that a new five year lease be drawn up at $190,000 per year, an increase of $56,000. I protested vehemently, since I simply did not have an extra $56,000 appropriated to me by the Legislature to take care of an increase. I had no desire to appear before a legislative committee and ask for a supplementary appropriation. I began to wonder whether that option had been allowed to lapse by accident or by intent. I protested the situation publicly during October and the first week of November but my timing was bad since it was the election period and my protests took place three weeks before the election. In addition, the Director of Administration was my opponent for re-election to the office of Secretary of State. The news media was understandably skeptical about my protestations. I think they suspected that this was all campaign oratory when I charged the Director of the Department of Administration with trying to sell me a sweetheart contract in this new lease at $190,000 per year. However, I had no choice in my timing, since the new lease had to be negotiated and at that time. Nevertheless, I refused to accept the proposed lease terms and simply moved the State Department offices out of that building to a new location in north Lansing in a supermarket grocery store. At any rate, a year later in October of 1967, I thought it was a good time to have a proposed grand jury take a hard look at state government.

A fourth area which I thought needed inspection was the Grand Duchy of Mackinac. The official name for this group is the Mackinac Island Commission, consisting of seven members, many of whom have served under both Republican and Democratic Governors who made the appointments. The interesting thing about the Commission was that they functioned almost completely autonomously. They granted leases and issued contracts with no other supervision from state government. Indeed, I was surprised to find that when they granted leases for property on the island, these leases were never submitted to the State Administrative Board for approval. I had been of the opinion that all leases must receive their final approval from the highest authority of the state, the State Administrative Board. Roger Lane of the *Detroit Free Press* writing about the Grand Duchy described the situation most eloquently.

LANSING—The tides of time and adversity washed over ancient Greece, the Roman Empire, the House of Hapsburg and other great dynasties.

And now, the hour may be late for the ruling authority of the Grand Duchy of Mackinac Island, the island State Park Commission, nurturer and exploiter of area history, conservator of horse-and-buggy era elegance, womb of spectacular vendettas, and many other things in its 40 years.

This most quaint and colorful of state agencies seems in peril of being overtaken by swift and fundamental changes in Michigan affairs—a new constitution, the vastly swollen and reorganized bureaucracy in Lansing and a stringent new code of official conduct.

As befits its princely estate, the seven-member commission at times has shown royalty's impatience with trifles and annoying regulations suited more to commoners.

The problem-solving genius of Commissioner W.F. Doyle has worked the agency out of resulting jams off and on for 28 years. The latest combination of obstacles could prove an insurmountable barrier to the commission's free-wheeling traditions.

The Commission has now, astonishingly, thumbed its nose at Michigan's attorney general, something that even Gov. Romney doesn't do.

The state officials ignored formal written advice that the award of a proposed 20-year property lease would violate a constitutional injunction, and that under the 1965 State Government Reorganization Act, their leasing discretion has been subordinated to policies set by the State Conservation Commission.

They also overrode privately given counsel urging postponement of pending lease decisions.

The basic issue is not one of crookedness, but one of sound

public policy in banishing at once the temptation, the opportunity or even the appearance of being open to bribery or improper invulence.

The common questionable thread in the contracting situations, and others on tap, boils down to this: in varying degrees, commissioners vote on arrangements affecting their private interests.

At a rockbottom minimum, four of the seven rent or lease, for nominal sums, state property entrusted to commission management. Two others have ownership or policy setting roles in commercial enterprises doing business with the commission.

These items and several more, I submitted to Governor Romney during the first weeks of October 1967, with copies to the Attorney General's office, and requested that the proposed grand jury be opened to all state departments. On the 24th of October the Governor acknowledged four communications on this subject and rejected my plea. The last paragraph of his letter to me was the clincher and I quote it in full.

I would suggest that if you feel that the information which you have is sufficient to form the basis for a Grand Jury investigation that you take upon yourself the task of filing the necessary petition. In addition, should our request for a Grand Jury be granted it will be up to the Grand Juror to ascertain the areas of investigation. If at this time you have any facts which you deem pertinent to the inquiry or the broadening of the inquiry, you should make them available to the Grand Juror.

His letter to me, of course, was the *coup de grace* and ended my hopes of widening the scope of the proposed grand jury. I had no attorneys within my jurisdiction to prepare the necessary legal papers. Once again, the full control of all attorneys by the Attorney General's office was an insurmountable obstacle.

I cannot blame Governor Romney for his rejection of my request. I suspect he thought this was a political ploy to open up the grand jury to inspect the departments over which he had authority and control, or he may have thought that I was simply trying to complicate an already complicated situation and defer the highway grand jury.

Once the decision was made to have a grand jury, the question became what court would conduct it. Eight months later, on June 4, the State Court of Appeals ruled that it was without authority to conduct an investigation of the State Highway Department. The vote was six to three. Finally, on June 19, 1968, the Ingham County Court agreed to conduct the grand jury investigation and, by the end of August, was beginning to hear its first witnesses. Circuit Court Judge Marvin J. Salmon was acting as Grand Juror. On June 17 of 1969, Judge Salmon reported his findings. He vindicated the seven year administration of John Mackie and personally filed a statement with the court attesting to Mackie's innocence. One man was indicted. He had been a former official in the Highway Department but had resigned in 1963. Another group of less than a dozen were roundly criticized, but not indicted.

This experience soured me to grand juries in general. I believe they have several very apparent defects. First, the period between the first accusative state, which is usually rumor and innuendo, and the actual calling of the grand jury, usually takes several years. During this period some innocent persons have their reputations ruined. Secondly, in the period before the grand jury actually begins, there is a political battlefield in which accusations of political chicanery go back and forth between the accused and the accusers. Third, when things are definitely wrong, it takes too long to get the show underway. Governor Romney's first questioning of the Highway Department took place in 1963, and it was not until 1969 that the Grand Jury was terminated. During much of this time, there was political infighting going on. Certainly John Mackie, an innocent administrator, was badly bruised over that period of time before his final vindication.

There is a better way. It is a governmental operation that has been tried successfully in other parts of the world for over a hundred years.

The idea: Import a novel Swedish institution created under a monarchy and strengthened in recent decades by a Socialist Government. It is called an Ombudsman, literally translated as representative's man, but more commonly referred to as a grievance man or watchdog of the people. In simple terms, an Ombudsman is a clearinghouse for complaints. Politically independent, he is given full powers of investigation to snip through red tape and make recommendations when he thinks a person was mistreated, or a decision wrong or based on incorrect or incomplete facts. Although he cannot reverse a decision, his recommendations are usually followed. In Sweden, in fact, he can prosecute officials and even judges.

It was initiated in Sweden in 1809 and has since been successfully tried in Finland, Denmark, Norway, New Zealand and Great Britain. The Ombudsman must be a remarkable person. He must be of impeccable reputation; a man of experience in Government; a non-political person who foregoes any connection with the political parties; he must be given a long enough term to be effective (in some countries he serves eight years, in others even longer) he must swear to forego any desire to return to politics or to run for further public office. Usually this means that the person selected for the office is a man past middle age, who will go into retirement after the completion of his term as an Ombudsman. He functions in a very different way from a Grand Jury. An Ombudsman can prevent injustices against a civil servant by another at a higher level. He can help citizens who feel they have no protection against arrogance and delay on the part of public officials. An individual complaint can be given quick relief. The office keeps public officials alert because they realize that a single incident of misfeasance can be exposed. But the greatest virtue of the Ombudsman office is that it can move quickly and effectively and the long period of waiting while building a petition for a grand jury is not necessary. The country which initiated the Ombudsman concept, Sweden, is about the same in population as Michigan. Why not give it a trial in Michigan?

V

THE LOBBYIST

IN the political world there is a quartet of words which have negative connotations. They are: Spoils System, Patronage, Slush Funds and Lobbyists. Now I shall take a look at the Lobbyists. The Dictionary of American Politics defines lobbies as "the main corridor of a capitol frequented by persons interested in legislation." Hence the extension, "the persons collectively whether principals or agencies who appear before legislative bodies or any of its committees to seek to influence individual members in order to accomplish the passage or defeat of bills." Since much of the persuasion used by lobbyists is done in back rooms, quietly over lunch tables or in the inner office of a legislator, the inference is often made that they are a sinister group. From time to time they are much maligned in the press. The people who lose in the legislative battlefield often attribute the defeat of their plans to the lobbyist. However, in general, lobbyists serve a very good purpose. They are working for their respective companies, unions or associations and they are usually very knowledgeable in their field. If any person in the executive offices of government needs to know the facts about a controversial situation, they have only to talk with the lobbyists on both sides of the question. They may not give him the full truth of the matter, but what they do reveal will be true and factual.

Michigan law requires that any person who attempts to influence the members of the Legislature, if they are paid for that particular duty, must register as a "legislative agent"—a very nice name for a lobbyist. He pays five dollars for the privilege of registering and a list is made of all registered lobbyists which is free to the public and to the legislators who make very good use of it. At the present time, I believe, there are more than two hundred lobbyists in the Michigan Capitol. The groups they represent are a cross section of Michigan and indeed, of American life. Just to name a few of those who are listed: American Airlines, Building Trades Council, Dow Chemical, Michigan Hospital Association, the Nurserymen, Michigan Bar Association, Blue Shield, AFL-CIO, Council on Alcoholic Problems, Michigan Automobile Dealers Association, Detroit Chamber of Commerce, Detroit Teachers' Federation, Automobile Club of Michigan, Life Underwriters, Chiropractic Physiotherapy Association, Credit Union League, The School Administrators, The City of Detroit, Detroit Retirement System, Distilleries Operators Institute, Funeral Directors, Michigan Trucking Association, Michigan Manufacturers Association, The Ford Motor Company.

The lobbyists, as a group, are intelligent men and women who usually come out of the particular association, union or corporation which they represent. Some of them represent groups wanting substantial change which the legislative chambers can give them. For example, more money to teachers, higher interest rates for the loan companies, permission to race greyhounds by some of the race tracks, or permission to move wider mobile homes on the highways. On the other hand, there is a group primarily interested in keeping things as they are and attempt to defeat change. These include the insurance companies who want no part of the "no fault" insurance; chambers of commerce representatives who oppose higher taxes; automobile companies who oppose some of Ralph Nader's recommendations for car safety; or the groups who oppose going to Daylight Savings Time.

In Michigan, the lobbyists are not required to disclose what spending they do in their efforts, but in many other states they are required by law to give a monthly, semi-annual or annual accounting of all monies spent in pursuing their particular interests. However, in Michigan, by law, the Legislature can subpoena the records of a Lobbyist and ascertain the amount of money spent in lobbying. In my memory, this has never been done. Nevertheless, I have always thought the spending of Michigan's lobbyists was moderate. They picked up the tab for many luncheons and dinners with legislators or other parties interested in the bill they were sponsoring. In addition, some associations give an annual party attended by most state officials and legislators. This very often takes place early in the session, and the first two months of each year the dinner schedule for a legislator is a hectic one.

Occasionally, a lobbyist hits the newspapers and the public records. Such was the case with the lobbyist for the PCHA (Peoples Community Hospital Authority), a little known agency which is the third largest hospital operation in Michigan. In 1965, when the story broke, this Authority owned four hospitals in Wayne, Trenton, Allen Park and Ypsilanti. Although these hospitals are private, they also received a subsidy of four-tenths of a mill property tax levy by terms of the legislative act from each community which enters the Authority. The Authority had been successful in obtaining federal funds to aid in the costs of building three of the four hospitals, and were hopeful of getting more in the future. All of this, of course, required a liaison between the Hospital Authority and the State Legislature and between the Authority and the Federal Government. It was revealed that the lobbyist for the PCHA had spent $186,000 over a ten year period in his lobbying activities, some in the entertainment of legislators and some for the expenses of the Authority directors at conventions such as the Michigan Hospital Association Convention at Mackinac Island. The average of seventeen thousand dollars per year in lobbying was probably not excessive in comparison to some of the lobbyists' spending by the major associations. However, the fact that the Authority was partially subsidized by tax money caused quite a political furor.

A case much closer to home for me was Senate Bill 1518, which surfaced in 1970. Early in that year, Otto Wendel, legislative liaison for the Teamsters Union, announced that he would attempt, in the legislature, to change the standards for driver licensing so that commercial drivers, such as the over-the-road truckers, would be allowed to have two separate drivers licenses, personal and commercial. Wendel had been very active as a lobbyist in the legislature for many years and was well known to at least one-third of the membership. He argued that those who drive for a living should be entitled to have more points against them under the law requiring persons with twelve or more points to be reexamined for their right to drive. After Wendel announced his intentions, I was not particularly concerned because I was sure that any law giving special privileges to a single class of drivers would have little chance in the Legislature. Little did I know.

On March 26, his bill was introduced into the Senate by Senator Charles Zollar and, on May 14, an identical bill was introduced in the House by Representative Al Sheridan. On May 20, the Senate bill was forced out of the Committee on Highways over the opposition of the chairman, James Fleming. By this time, I was issuing public statements opposing the dual license concept. I argued, first, that for all practical purposes this would mean that any driver with both an operators and chauffeurs license would be given the privilege of having at least twenty-four points against him before he would be cited. Secondly, one license might be suspended or revoked but the other would still be valid. This was particularly dangerous when a license was revoked for drunk driving, hit-and-run driving or using a car in the commission of a felony. On June 2, the bill passed the Senate by a twenty-six to nine vote. Now it was up to the House to move, and the Appropriations Committee met on June 11 to consider Bill 1518. Attending to oppose the bill were Representative Raymond Schmitt, Captain Richard Plants, now Head of the State Police, Sergeant William Hook, Frank DeRose from the Governor's office, Milo Chalfant, Harold Kimmel, Harley Neideffer and Jack Eno from our office. Prior to the meeting, Representative Kehres made the statement to those opposing the bill, with the exception of Representative Smitt, to "Keep your mouth shut unless questioned and then only answer the questions." He further stated he was conveying the wishes of the Speaker, William Ryan. Needless to say, this meeting was reported in the newspapers within a week, and did nothing to help the image of the bill. The Appropriations Committee voted to support the bill.

Incidentally, the Teamsters Agent, Otto Wendel, was allowed to sit at the committee table along with the other representatives. This is a rather unusual situation.

Public opposition to the bill grew and there was much editorial comment opposing it. Every traffic safety organization in the state went on record in opposition. In fact, there seemed to be no one in favor of the bill other than the Teamsters Union and the legislators themselves. On June 9, Noel Buffe, Director of the Office of Highway Safety Planning in the Governor's office, asked Douglas Toms, Director of the National Highway Safety Bureau in the Department of Transportation, for his opinion on the bill. The response was that this bill would be in violation of the national safety standards issued in 1967, which required that each state shall have a program which provides that each driver hold only one license. I might say that the original intent of that part of the standard was to keep drivers from having a license in several states. It was inconceivable to the National Safety Board that any state would issue two licenses in one state to one person. However, on June 23, the bill passed the House by a narrow margin, fifty-six to forty-one. Finally, on July 7, the enrolled bill was presented to the Governor for consideration. The question then became how could a bill that had no public support whatsoever go through both Houses in the Legislature? Radio station WJR, in a newscast of July 9, threw some light on that subject: "Republican Representative Quincy Hoffman of Applegate who opposed the bill says Wendel offered him campaign help if he could vote for the bill. Representative James Tierney of Garden City, a Democrat, says he was told organized labor, the UAW as well as the Teamsters, would run a candidate against him in the Primary if he voted against the bill." At this point, I put out a facetious press release suggesting that the Aeronautics Commission should allow pilots one free fatality crash before they were investigated.

Meanwhile, Representative Quincy Hoffman, who had formerly been a sheriff and a strong traffic safety advocate, and Robert Waldron, Minority Leader of the House, sent a petition to the Governor with almost fifty signatures on it asking that the Governor veto the bill and promising that with these signatures he could uphold a veto. The opposition continued, practically all newspapers editorialized against the bill and urged a veto, and all safety organizations in the state sent in resolutions to the same effect. Finally on July 15, Governor Milliken, with substantial political courage in an election year, veoted the bill.

Throughout the entire controversy, there were two ironies surfacing from time to time. First, the people to whom the bill would have given special privileges did not need that kind of help. As a group, they are the safest drivers in the world, and the Michigan Trucking Association gives annual awards to the best drivers in this group. Many of them have driven hundreds of thousands of miles without a violation or accident. I spoke to several of them at a banquet given in their honor, and was told, "Hell no, we don't need this bill. It certainly wasn't for us." The only publicity that any member of the Teamsters Union other than Otto Wendel received was a letter to the Public Letter Box in the Lansing Journal. This letter was written by a member of the Teamster Local 337 of Lansing, and the writer indicated he had been a member of the union for eighteen years. He gave the usual reasons in support of the bill and argued that anyone who drives for a living should be given special consideration. Just for fun, we looked up his driving record and his recent computer tape showed five accidents plus three moving violations.

The aftermath of the Governor's veto of the Teamsters Bill was interesting because it highlighted the fact that Otto Wendel, highpowered, well-financed and influential, was still not an officially and legally registered lobbyist. The *Jackson Citizen Patriot* had this to say under the headline "Teamster Lobbyist angered by Veto":

> The perils of a lobbyist are many and the worst that can happen is to have a governor veto one of his bills. That's what happened last week to Teamster lobbyist Otto Wendel, a heavy handed crusader for extra benefits for Michigan truck drivers, whose motto is 'you're either with me or against me' and no middle ground.
> Governor William G. Milliken grounded the effusive Wendel

a few days ago by vetoing legislation that would allow truck drivers two operator's licenses.

Wendel, who has not registered as a lobbyist under state law, screamed loudly and promised political retaliation against the governor at the polls next Movember. Some legislators screamed just as loudly at Wendel's lobbying techniques and the noise reached the office of the Attorney General Frank J. Kelley, who is trying to find out why Wendel did not register as a lobbyist.

The governor said, in his veto message, the legislation would be a backward step in traffic safety.

Wendel immediately said the veto is a backward step in the political future of Governor Milliken.

He has acquired from the executive office the pen with which the veto message was written, along with the text, and now plans to put the two together in a broadside to be delivered to 50,000 to 60,000 truck drivers in the state, and to thousands of other holders of chauffeurs' licenses. The bill would have permitted holders of chauffeurs' and operators licenses to accumulate 24 points in a two year period before losing either license. Private motorists are permitted only 12 points.

'I wish,' said Wendel, 'we had a picture of the governor's hand as he signed the veto message. That would help. This is going out not only to members of the teamsters but to other units which represent cab drivers and bus drivers and others who make a living by driving.'

Governor Milliken's office did not panic at the news that Wendel will go after the governor with the consolation prize— the free pen. Aides are certain no attempt will be made to override the governor's veto when the lawmakers return for a brief session early in August.

Wendel was more concerned about the manner in which the press handled the affair that he was in the investigation by the attorney general into why he has not registered as a lobbyist.

'The press mangled and misrepresented the entire affair' he said. 'Nobody understood the purpose of the bill but the safety organizations in the state made a big thing out of it. I have rebutted every argument they made for it.'

He said he will not make a formal statement on the attorney general's investigation until he talks with his attorneys.

'I doubt that I will register as a lobbyist,' he declared. 'I am a Teamster's union official and I was told by my lawyers that I didn't have to. If everyone else registers I may also. There are many people around the Legislature who have not registered, so why should I?'

A month later Attorney General Kelley entered the fray and responded to questions concerning why Teamsters' Representative Otto Wendel was not prosecuted for operating as a lobbyist when he was not registered as such. He issued the following statement:

> On August 16, 1962, concluding a 28-page report of an investigation of lobbying, I made the following observation:
>> The present lobbying law is almost completely useless, ineffectual, inadequate and worthless. It neither regulates nor licenses, nor does it provide for the disclosure of any information of value.
> In another part of the report, the following was said:
>> Every year or two the citizenry is alerted by a particularly outrageous foray by some of the lobbyists but as the crisis passes so does the public interest. This report is dedicated to the hope that the people of our State will recognize the great need for meaningful action to prevent serious abuse of our legislative process and will act accordingly.
> It is a sad fact that today—over eight years later—both quotations can be repeated word for word and that they still retain their full meaning and effect.
> Not a single change has been made in the lobbying law during this period. Nor have the problems highlighted by the investigation and report of 1962 been altered.
> The latest expression of concern relates to an individual who is not registered as a lobbyist but who expressed his views concerning pending legislation to members of the legislature. Questions were raised as to whether action could be taken against him for his activities since he was not registered.
> This is not a new problem. During the entire history of the so-called Legislative Agents Act, large groups of persons have declined to register contending that they are not required to do so because they do not fall within the statutory definition of a legislative agent. The statute defines a legislative agent as:
>> * * * a person *who is employed* by a person, firm, association,

or corporation; or by any board, department, or agency of the state of Michigan, or any political subdivision thereof, *to engage* in promoting, advocating, or opposing any matter pending before either house of the legislature or any committee thereof, or *who is employed expressly* for the purpose of promoting, advocating, or opposing any matter which might legally come before either house of the legislature or any committee thereof. (Emphasis supplied).

But it exempts:

Any person who shall confine his activities in promoting, advocating or opposing any matter pending before either house of the legislature or any committee thereof, to written communications or to formal appearances before any legislative committee or committees to which such matter has been duly referred, and who in writing clearly identifies himself to the committee together with each and every person, firm, association, corporation, or other interest represented by him, shall not be deemed to be a legislative agent within the meaning of this act; neither shall such term include any person whose contact with the legislature is limited to furnishing information at the request of any legislator or legislative committee regarding any matter pending before either house of the legislature or any committee thereof.

Any close examination makes it clear that the definition of a legislative agent in the present law is as full of holes as Swiss cheese. In addition, the exemption provision is so vague and all-inclusive as to give all kinds of persons an excuse for not registering.

Many individuals who have engaged in discussing pending legislation with members of the legislature are not (in the words of the statute) '*employed* * * * *to engage* in promoting, advocating, or opposing * * *' pending legislation. They contend and some have been advised by counsel that they are not required to be registered since they are not 'employed * * * to engage' in lobbying. Some are elected officials of their organizations whose main duties relate to their elected post and whose duties only incidentally require them to be in touch with the legislature from time to time. Others are employees of governmental agencies who are also not involved in dealing with the legislature except incidentally.

In these circumstances, and given the loophole-filled definition of legislative agent and the principle that penal statutes must be strictly construed, plus the constitutional guarantee of freedom of speech, it would be impossible in the most recent case, as it would in almost any other case imaginable, to require these individuals to register, much less to prosecute an individual under this law who is not clearly, specifically *employed* for the purpose of lobbying.

This is an intolerable situation. The public interest is mocked by a law which appears to be serving an important public need but, in reality, by its existence, paralyzes needed efforts to establish effective regulation of lobbying activities.

I wonder if the public realizes what is at stake here. As was pointed out in the lobbying report in 1962, ' * * * lobbyists have a greater proportion of influence with some legislators in the passage of the public laws of this State than that possessed by any individual citizen or group of citizens not represented by an active lobbyist.'

The best way of rectifying the situation is to provide for regulation of lobbying activities. This the present law does not do, and history has shown that the legislature is not interested in taking that step. Only if there is an unprecedented demand and continual expressions of public concern can sufficient pressure be brought to bear so that adequate legislation will be passed.

I therefore call again for a new lobbying law, regulating the practice in the public interest and requiring that *all* who are engaged in lobbying be required to register, whether they are specifically employed for that purpose or not. The only exemption that should be made is for an individual who is specifically required by the legislature to express his or her viewpoint on pending legislation, or where a citizen, not representing any particular organization, limits his activities to written communications or to formal appearances before a legislative committee.

I continue to believe that this legislation should include the following major provisions:

A. Lobbyists would be licensed by the State.

B. The license would be based on a joint application by the lobbyist and his employer setting forth full information concerning their relationship and the background of the lobbyist.

C. A provision for a public filing of regular monthly accounts by the lobbyist setting forth all direct or indirect expenditures in money, services, or anything of value made directly or indirectly to any state legislator. This would include all expenses.

D.   A provision for the semi-annual public filing of an account by the lobbyist's employer setting forth all expenditures of whatever nature made in regard to lobbying.

E.   A provision for the suspension or revocation of the lobbyist's license for certain specified reasons, including:

1.   Failure to file prescribed reports;

2.   Filing false reports;

3.   Directly or indirectly furnishing goods or services of pecuniary value to a state legislator; and

4.   The violation of any provision of the act.

F.   A provision for criminal penalties for lobbying without a license, failing to file required reports, or filing false reports.

G.   A provision more clearly defining the scope of the act and exemptions from it in order to avoid any questions concerning its impact.

H.   A provision granting authority to the Attorney General to investigate and prosecute violations of the act and granting to him the power, upon application in each case to a circuit court, to subpoena individuals and records.

I call upon the people of this state, and the news media, to let their voices be heard in a demand for such legislation.

I hope that eight years from now an Attorney General will not be required to refer back to this report and to the report which was issued in 1962 and say of the lobbying law and of the lack of public concern what I have said earlier in this report: 'It is a sad fact that today—over eight (16) years later—both quotations can be repeated word for word and that they still retain their full meaning and effect.'

I think, on balance, the lobbyists are very reputable people who are honestly needed. Certainly they must be publicly identified as such so that members of the government including the Governor, will know who they are. Certainly the Teamster bill was no example of how they usually work. As a group, their efforts are made very unobtrusively and in an intelligent fashion. Many times I have thought they were more to be pitied than to be criticized, when I see them at the mercy of the politicians. Since their names are open to the public, they receive invitations to every testimonial dinner given by any politician running for office, and they are in the most delicate position of either buying the necessary tickets which may be ten or fifty dollars each, or going on the black list of that particular politician. What a choice!

One incident in the controversy will always remain in my mind, that is the action of Representative James Tierney when he signed the letter requesting the Governor to veto the bill. Tierney had taken a great deal of pressure because of his opposition to the bill and when he signed the request letter, his signature was at least twice as large as any one of the other fifty. It was a real "John Hancock."

VI

PATRONAGE-POLITICAL
OR OTHERWISE

THE definition of political patronage is, according to the Dictionary of American Politics, "the power to make appointments to office, especially when not governed by Civil Service laws or rules, also the power to grant contracts and various special favors." In my opinion, this definition is a bit narrow.

During the nine years I taught political science at Wayne State University, I took a rather dim view of political patronage. In fact, I am afraid I conveyed to my students the belief that there was something a bit tainted about it. I was a strong believer in the complete Civil Service system. My colleagues, in the Political Science Department, pretty much shared this viewpoint, and also conveyed it to their students. When I became actively involved in politics, at the beginning of the 1950's, I had somewhat modified my viewpoint, probably due to the practicalities demanded of a person in politics. At any rate, I now take the view that a case can be made both for political patronage and the Civil Service system. Indeed, I believe that there are certain circumstances in which a Civil Service system does not work very well and that the political patronage system works much better. In fact, I believe that there are three specific kinds of situations in which the patronage system works substantially better than a Civil Service system would.

The first situation is where a member of the executive branch must have a person or persons who will help make policy and/or put it into effect. Under those circumstances he must have a free-wheeling choice of the type of people he wants to appoint. I think there is no argument with this particular situation. All the experts are agreed that it makes good sense.

The second situation which justifies patronage is where a patronage system can operate more efficiently or more economically than any other kind. The critical reader at this point may argue that this is impossible. But the facts of governmental life are that there are a fair number of situations where a patronage system is substantially cheaper to operate than anything else that has been devised.

A third rationale for the political patronage system comes from the side effects. Since recipients of patronage know that they are appointed by reason of their activities in their political party, or in behalf of a particular candidate, they know and expect to make political contributions and it is accepted. The net result is that substantial amounts of the total campaign contributions received by a party, or by a candidate, are those that are received from people who are getting political patronage.

At this point, the political purists will argue that this is a defect and not an argument for political patronage. However, in the practicalities of politics, it turns out to have a very beneficial effect. Those who make the contributions, and the persons who receive them, acknowledge them publicly. They become a part of the public record and are reported at the end of a campaign. This, in my opinion, is its great virtue. Contrast this method of raising funds for a candidate with what goes on in other areas of campaign fund solicitations—often anonymous, often questionable. Therefore, I would argue that anything that exposes the source of campaign contributions is a virtue and that, almost by accident, this becomes an argument for political patronage.

One item I must hasten to clarify is that the recipients of political patronage do not necessarily receive fees or salaries. Indeed, some of those most sought after are unpaid jobs, but are in reality *prestige* jobs. These appointments may be made on merit alone, but they too have side effects in that they may enable the recipient of that patronage to indirectly profit in his business, his profession, or his union.

There is a tendency on the part of people in politics to play down the patronage side of government. In fact, from time to time I would read an item in the newspaper stating that the Secretary of State's office was the last department of state government that had a large remnant of patronage within it. Needless to say, this was far from the full truth. The reason it occurred was that I not only publicly acknowledged that it was political patronage, but indeed I defended it as being a more economical method to pursue the work of our department. My colleagues on the State Administrative Board in the late 1950's used to tease me about this. My answer was there are at least two of you whom I would be very happy to trade patronage with. That usually ended the discussion. They wanted no part of that kind of a trade.

To better understand patronage I would like to spell out in some detail the patronage that does take place in the various departments of government. Since the Secretary of State's office is the one that is most prominently mentioned in the newspapers, I will start with that. First of all, the Secretary has the power to appoint five deputies, whose job it is both to help formulate policy and to carry it out. In addition, the Secretary is authorized by law to appoint the managers of the various local license plate offices scattered throughout the state. The manager receives his compensation in fees; thirty cents per plate sale. He transfers titles, sells boat plates and, in general, is a counsellor in his neighborhood for anyone who had automotive transactions to make. Out of the fees he receives, he has to rent a building, keep it clean, heat it, light it and provide telephone service. In addition, he has to hire any additional personnel that he might need.

The majority of these managerships become family affairs, or as we call them, momma-poppa arrangements, in which the whole family works in the license bureau. When the rush period comes other help is hired. Since the sale of license plates tends to be a boom and bust affair, an office might fluctuate from a single person working in it to six or seven people during the rush period. This flexibility, of course, is its great virtue. There is no reason for having a set number of persons working all year and, indeed, the employment in the office can fluctuate during the day and in accordance with the weather. As a result it is a substantially more economical system to run from the taxpayers standpoint. Lest the reader think that these patronage appointments are only for political reasons, I hasten to point out that every other state in the country uses essentially the same system to sell license plates.

These managers do not receive any of the rewards of a Civil Service system. There is no pension at the end of their tenure; there are no vacation benefits; no unemployment compensation benefits and, worst of all, no social security. Small wonder that this system is substantially cheaper to operate than a Civil Service system. Side by side, within the system, there are also twelve or thirteen Civil Service offices that are doing exactly the same work. This gave me an opportunity to see how the costs of the two compared. I found that the patronage system, in this particular kind of a situation, cost approximately half the amount that a Civil Service system would have cost under the same circumstances.

The patronage appointments turned out to be very individualistic and rugged entrepreneurs, and the competition between offices became very rough and tough at times. One would not think when people are selling an identical product—a license plate—for identical money, that there would be much chance for salesmanship. But of course the service item was the important differential offered by the various offices. One manager competed so strongly that, working out of Pontiac, he was able to sell plates to truck fleets in Muskegon. Needless to say, when one manager encroached on the territory of another we were called upon to arbitrate. I usually simply stuck to the *laissez faire* policy.

Very often the manager operates the license plate bureau out of his own private business. That office might be an insurance agency or an automobile accessory store. Certainly the great number of people who pass through the license office increases his sales in his own private business. In the smaller towns the offices might be in a home or a gas station, and in those towns the rewards are so small it is quite difficult to find anybody to take the job.

The offices vary in size. Some of them have fees of only a few hundred dollars a year, while others would be substantially above $25,000 a year. Approximately half of the managers receive $6,000 or less per year, which is certainly not overpaying anyone for running a shop forty hours a week, fifty two weeks a year. In fact, I often wondered whether or not, in some cases, we were paying substantially less than the legal minimum wage.

There are two other ways in which the branch managers are able to help their financial situation. One way is notarizing documents, for which they are allowed to charge fifty cents. The other, is to sell nuts and bolts to the motorists purchasing license plates. The two items together, in the hands of a manager who is a good salesman, can be quite a lucrative thing. In fact, several managers have told me that all their campaign contributions were paid for out of the proceeds from these two items.

This brings us to the specific story of campaign contributions on the part of patronage recipients. No part of the political spectrum has been more maligned, misunderstood and misinterpreted than campaign contributions on the part of these appointees. To begin with, the two hundred and ten managers that I had at any one time were persons who had applied for the job to their county Democratic committee. After a search of their credit background, their references and their police record, I made the appointment. Of the several hundred appointments I made over a sixteen year period, I only knew a half a dozen of them before the time of their appointment. When they applied to the county committee for recommendation for the job in their county, they assured that county committee that they would make contributions to the party comparable to the income they received. It never came as a shock to them, when election years rolled around, that they were expected to make a contribution.

I soon found, after coming into office, that the one thing that they were concerned about was that their contribution would be on a par with that of another manager who was earning approximately the same income. If they thought, or believed, that they were paying more than their fair share then rebellion made itself manifest very quickly. During the first five of my years in office, the Democratic State Central Committee did the collecting of the campaign funds. But it did not work out fairly or evenly. Some of them got off the hook with hard luck stories; others stalled on their payments until the election was over and they were sure of retaining their job. This helped the candidates not at all. Others postponed payment until after the rush period and then resigned.

This kind of chaos became intolerable, and the branch managers came to me and asked that a new method of collection be set up. This resulted in the formation of the Michigan Branch Managers Association. There were officers and regional chairmen. It became their job to work out a scale of contributions which would be fair to all. Even more important, this scale was known to all of them, so that they did not have the feeling that they were giving too much and the man in the next town was giving too little.

To start with, it was decided by the officers of the Branch Managers Association that those who earned in fees $5,000 or $6,000 a year would make no contribution at all, but would be expected to buy one annual ticket to the Jeff-Jack Day Dinner. Those earning over $6,000 a year gave on a sliding scale which not only took in account the fees they received from the state, but also a guesstimate of what they took in on notary public fees, payment for nuts and bolts, as well as what the branch office did for the branch managers' own private business.

In the case of a man running, for instance, an auto accessory shop, he might increase his profit for a year by $10,000 if he were also a branch manager. Through the Association the branch managers were able to police themselves and collect the contributions. As a result of this kind of an agreement, ninety-five percent of the branch managers cooperated extremely well, and the chaos of the previous years was ended.

I remember very well a Democratic Party dinner at which Senator Sander Levin was the guest of honor. He was the recipient of two checks totalling some $70,000 from the Branch Managers Association. Part of the money was to go to the State Central Committee and part to the Democratic County Committees. The checks were handed over to Levin by the Branch Managers Association Chairman, Kelley O'Callaghan, who was at that time a branch manager in Muskegon. O'Callaghan had worked very long and hard in working out a fair and equitable scheme of raising the funds from the total group of branch managers and they were well satisfied with the formula for collection. Later on he was to become one of my very valued deputies.

As always, there were a few, certainly not over three or four in any one year, who tried to get out of making their contribution, or at least to cut it down. They had all sorts of hard luck stories to tell, but the managers themselves kept them pretty much in line. Under the new Association policy, the total contributions increased from $35,000 a year to somewhat over $100,000 toward the end of my tenure of office. I recall the manager coming in to see me about nine weeks before an election and saying he was not going to make a contribution to the party. He bluntly stated that, if I attempted to remove him, he would go to the television and the newspaper people and report we were putting the strong arm on him. I reminded him that when he got his job he had promised his county committee that he would make contributions. His only answer was "Yes, but that was two years ago, that isn't today." Knowing how well reporters might like to pick up this kind of a story, and having had some experience in the past with branch managers who were fired for either embezzlement or for discourtesy to their customers, I certainly did not want to take the formal drastic move of removing this particular manager from office. The solution really was not too difficult. I appointed a new manager, in a new location, less than five miles away from the reluctant one, and that cut into his business so badly that he resigned within six months. There is more than one way to skin a cat.

So much for patronage in the State Department. I think in general it worked out pretty well. Certainly it was much easier on the taxpayers than a Civil Service system. It was able to give better service to the people who needed it most, the auto dealers, than any forty hour Civil Service office. No automobile dealership would ever trade for a

Civil Service office, simply because the patronage offices keep longer hours, operate on Saturday or Sunday if need be. The automobile dealers appreciate this and give them their total patronage.

Now let us consider the Governor's office. This poor man, whether he be Democrat or Republican, has the most miserable job of all. He gets almost all the blame for things that go wrong, but he does not necessarily get the credit when things go right. He is frustrated by the Legislature, by the financial problems of the state, by the courts, and yet he is held responsible for all that transpires in state government. One of the few redeeming features of his job is the fact that he has literally hundreds of appointments to make. Some of these appointments are to administrative positions, a few are to policy making positions, but the great majority of them are to advisory boards and commissions.

Most of the administrative appointments are full time jobs, with rather good salaries attached. These include the sixteen principal department heads that he appoints. They have jobs that can either make or break the Governor's political future by the way they function. Some commissions, such as the Liquor Control Bureau, are full time jobs, and the members function both as policy makers and as administrators. Another type of commission is the Civil Service Commission, in which the members meet two or three days a month, and receive only their expenses. In this case, they function primarily as policy makers. Some of the commissions, like the Liquor Bureau and the Civil Service Commission, are required by law to be bi-partisan, and the Governor must keep a balance on those commissions between the two parties.

Then there are a host of boards and commissions that are advisory in nature. Some of them are very large, meet perhaps one day a month, and function in an advisory capacity to some executive in state government. A listing of those boards and commissions comes as a great surprise to most people who have no idea that many of them even exist. For instance: State Council for the Arts, The Michigan Public School Employees Retirement Board, The Commission for Agriculture, The Michigan Apple Commission, The State Racing Commission, The Michigan State Fair Authority, The Civil Rights Commission, The Aeronautics Bureau, The Cemetery Bureau, The Public Service Bureau, The Michigan Correction Commission, The Michigan Higher Education Assistance Authority, The State Higher Educational Facilities Commission, The State Board for Libraries, The State Tenure Commission, The Carnival Amusement Safety Board, The Ski Area Safety Board, The Wage Deviation Board, The Michigan State Athletic Board of Control, The State Board of Cosmetology, The Michigan State Board of Dentistry, The State Board of Horology, The Board of Marriage Counselors, The Board of Registration in Medicine, The Board of Examiners for Sanitariums.

The foregoing list gives some idea of the number and diversity of the appointments that the Governor must make. I believe that by the end of Governor Milliken's first two years in office, he had made some thirteen hundred appointments. Many of these boards and commission appointments are widely sought after. I think probably the most sought after one is the seven man Mackinac Island Park Commission. One of the rewards to the members who are appointed is that most of them end up living in a summer home on the Island.

By and large, the people who are appointed to these various boards and commissions, as well as to executive positions in state employment, are people who would do a very fine job in any capacity. Usually, they are people of influence in their occupation or their community. Certainly, most of them are grateful to the governor who makes the appointment. The vast majority of these appointees, come election year, remember the man who appointed them, and make contributions to his new campaign. Again I will argue that this is commendable. This is a forthright contribution, which is publicly acknowledged, and the motivation behind them known. Usually the Governor, before making an appointment, will clear it with the local political county committee and make sure that they would either recommend that person, or, at least, that they have no objection to the particular person involved. You will note that the kind of patronage in the State Department was very different from that in the Governor's office. The methods of compensation were different, and the duties of the recipients of the patronage were very different.

As we look at other offices, you will note that each office has its own distinctive, and different, kind of patronage. Take that of the office of the Attorney General.

The Attorney General is a constitutional officer. He is a member of the executive department of state government. He is the chief law enforcement officer of the state, and the head of the Department of the Attorney General. His duties are prescribed by law.

It follows that his patronage is, almost exclusively, with attorneys in private practice throughout the state. The Attorney General is legal counsel for the Legislature, and for the official departments, boards and commissions of state government. With this kind of responsibility, he has a very substantial staff of civil servants who are called Assistant Attorney Generals. All of them are members of the State Bar of Michigan.

However, the amount of work required by the Attorney General's office is far greater than the staff of Assistant Attorney Generals can handle. Therefore, subject to the Attorney General's approval, legal work is handed out to attorneys in private practice. A good example is the State Public Administrator, who is charged with the duty of administering all escheated estates, and represents the Attorney General on the Board of Escheats. The administration of these estates, where a property owner has died without leaving a will, is farmed out to the various attorneys throughout the state.

Another area (where I was personally interested) is the administration of the Michigan Motor Vehicle Accident Claims Fund. This is a fund set up by law to reimburse the victims of automobile accidents in which there is no other means of securing compensation for them. The fund is financed by contributions from motorists of $1.00, if then insured, and $35.00, if they are not insured, for liability at the time they purchase their license plates. In the course of the administration of the law, the numerous claims made by injured parties have to be scrutinized from a legal standpoint. The Attorney General appoints approximately forty attorneys from all over the state to handle these cases.

Parenthetically, the legal fraternity seems to be very anxious to handle this sort of legal procedure because I had numerous requests from attorneys asking that they be assigned cases. Since the Claims Fund had been set up in the Secretary of State's office, the attorneys involved thought I was also appointing the attorneys. This was far from the truth, of course, and I had to refer them to the Attorney General's office.

The attorneys who are appointed by the Attorney General to handle various kinds of cases for the state are given the designation of Special Assistant Attorney General. Needless to say, the vast majority of the attorneys appointed belong to the same political faith as the Attorney General of the moment. They tend to be attorneys who are politically active on the local government level and, as a group, they are very good and reasonable contributors to the political campaigns.

One of the little sidelights on the system is that very often a law firm, interested in securing legal business from the state, would be a partnership of one Republican and one Democrat. In that way, when a Republican Attorney General was in office, the Republican in the law firm would be the one who would ask for the business, and *vice versa* when the Democrats came into office.

As a group, the special assistants are at least moderately active politically at the local level and are good contributors to political campaigns. The penalty for failure to contribute, one attorney told me, is to see the flow of cases from the Attorney General soon dry up. Some special assistants earn more than $20,000 a year from such assignments, so few fail to take care of their political obligations.

The State Treasurer dispenses another form of patronage, one which he is compelled to use and which, basically, he can operate only through certain channels. It involves the custody, investment and disbursement of literally billions of dollars of state funds.

Within the Department of Treasury are some special divisions which handle the funds involved in what amounts to a form of fixed patronage. The Investment Division is custodian of the various trust and agency funds, the sinking funds, the pension and retirement funds and the operating funds. Its primary responsibility is investment of the funds in accordance with state law and, in some cases, the directives of trustees. The Banking Control Division receives and deposits all monies for the State of Michigan, its departments, boards, institutions and commissions, including federal grants in aid.

Thus, the State Treasurer is responsible for investing and/or depositing all the monies that come into state coffers and all the various funds. Like any wise custodian, with the interests of his client in mind, he aims for good interest, dividends and security. It is an awesome legal responsibility.

Tax money collected each year amounts to some two billion dollars. Pension funds account for another billion or more. At no one time does the State Treasurer have those three billion in his charge, because tax monies usually flow in and out within a few days. Nevertheless, several hundred million dollars are usually on hand.

The State Treasurer can deposit this money in banks; he can buy short-term notes; he can buy stocks and bonds and make other investments. He must always know the demands to be made on any fund or account so that it is fluid enough to take care of its obligations. But —a fact little known to the general public—investment of money in the State Treasurer's charge will earn as much as seventy-five million a year.

Given these circumstances, it is natural that hosts of people are willing to help the Treasurer safeguard and invest the money he controls. These include almost any banker in the state, as well as brokers with offerings of stocks and bonds. The Treasurer consequently makes deposits in more than three hundred banks in the state, the amount depending on the size of the bank, its capitalization, the security it provides and the interest it will pay. Amounts deposited range from a few thousand dollars in a small bank to twenty million dollars or more in the largest banks.

Needless to say, the banks are happy to get this money and are grateful to the department of state government that makes the deposits. Investment of money in stocks or bonds or notes produces like gratitude from the brokerage houses and the salesmen who benefit.

Two personal experiences exemplify the nature of the response. In 1957, a vice president of one of the largest banks in Michigan called me to report that the bank's board of directors had discussed adding a new director and wondered if I would be interested in becoming one. Of course I was flattered. I questioned privately whether it would put me into a conflict of interest, but asked for a week to consider the offer. Before the week was up, the banker called me again and said he understood the Secretary of State's office collected more than two hundred million dollars a year in taxes. He wondered what portion of that amount might be invested or deposited in his bank. I explained that I had nothing to do with investing the money—that was the responsibility of the State Treasurer. The conversation quickly terminated and I never heard from him or his bank again.

Several years ago, a man wandered into my office and identified himself as a banker from the western part of the state. He said he had recently become the beneficiary of a fairly large deposit from the State Treasurer and that this presented him with a problem.

"I know you're a Democrat," he said, "and I know I am receiving the money from a Republican administration. I'm embarrassed to go to the Republicans and ask them how I should express my thanks, so I came to you for advice."

Concealing my amusement, I suggested to him that he could respond by purchasing a few tickets to the annual Republican Lincoln Day dinner that was about to take place in his area. He thanked me and left. I never saw him again, nor did I ever find out what he did for the Republican Party. Nevertheless, it was warming to know that some people were grateful for the rewards bestowed upon them, by whatever political party.

Patronage controlled by the State Treasurer is unique because he cannot escape it. He has no choice but to pick and choose who shall get what monies under what circumstances. The only alternative would be creation of a State Bank of Michigan to keep its own money and its own resources and make loans in competition with private banks. This, of course, is unthinkable.

So much for the four main avenues of patronage in state government. Some of my political colleagues think my views are too restricted, contending that I should recognize other forms of patronage not readily apparent. Some point to what they call civil servants patronage under which state employees determine which businesses benefit from their decisions. They argue, for example, that a purchasing agency is constantly selecting from among like items and simply throwing business one way or another. Some might thus benefit their friends to the exclusion of other businessmen. Another employee might write specifications for an item so that only one firm could submit a bid to furnish it to the state. I sensed this dilemma in my own department when we purchased highly expensive computer systems. My decision was to tell the technicians and executives involved to write the specifications and make the final judgments, since they were the ones who would have to live with the computers.

My colleagues point out too that the major state universities are autonomous, enabling their officials to indulge in what might be called academic patronage. The fiscal agent or treasurer in any large university controls as much as one hundred million dollars in any one year. Like state funds, the money must be invested and deposited. Like the State Treasurer, he can decide where the money goes.

The workings of the patronage system in Michigan demonstrate, I believe, that it can be of benefit to the people of the state. It is also apparent that, in terms of jobs or fees or business received, the beneficiaries number several thousand citizens. All are part of what the New Left calls the Establishment, but they are the unseen part of the Establishment, the large segment of the government iceberg that lies beneath the surface. For the most part, they are influential citizens, usually active in their communities and their political parties, and therefore important to the well-being of the state.

As a group, they are not amenable to changing the system to any large degree. This over-all attitude has great bearing on the future course of Government. It concerns me to some degree, because I believe that there are changes that need to be made. My proposals in that regard I will outline in another chapter.

Some of my former colleagues in Government, upon reading the rough draft of this chapter, point out that I have neglected a specific area which they title "Civil Service System Personnel Patronage." This, of course, is only a fancy name for the practice of hiring consultants in state government from outside the Civil Service system. These are contractual arrangements between the departments of state government and individuals who very often have other full-time jobs. Persons who are hired by contract work on specific projects, or codifications of law, or special research developments, or act as advisers to department heads. These contracts are of short duration, but are well remunerated and, at least theoretically, the persons hired are persons who cannot be found within the normal long-term tenure Civil Service system. It is possible under this particular facet of patronage to hire on a contractual basis, a full-time college faculty member or a retired governmental employee who has special knowledge and skills. On the other hand, it is equally possible that a person who has a particular personal "in" with high government officials may go from one contractual job to another over a period of years and thus essentially stay outside of the usual constrictions of the Civil Service system as it applies to the ordinary employees. From time to time some members of the Legislature object strenuously to the practice because it is a means by which the executive wing of government can pay out substantially more money in a consultant fees than they could do under the regular wage limits set by the Civil Service Commission. There have been cases when individuals were *persona non grata* to legislative committees and whose salary levels in the unclassified appointed positions were cut by legislative action, and yet the administrative departments of government have been able to get around the salary restriction by simply handing out consultants contracts to the individuals involved.

VII

THE SLUSH FUNDS

PRIVATE funds raised by the supporters of political office holders have many names—Flower Fund, Development Fund, Slush Fund, Off-Year Campaign Fund, and Incidentals Fund. I am going to use the name for this chapter, The Slush Fund, not because it has the worst connotation but because it is probably the most accepted name, unfortunate though it may be, to the general public. I also attempt to point out that a slush fund is not only inevitable but necessary in the life of any political office holder.

While writing this chapter, I read in the *Detroit News* that Mayor Gribbs is setting up a private "Mayor's Development Fund" and scheduling a dinner with fifty dollar tickets in hope of raising $70,000 for the fund. The story goes on to say that the private fund will be used for entertainment, political contributions, social activities and miscellaneous expenses of office that the City Council does not finance. This would include money to permit Mayor Gribbs and his wife to engage in a number of social functions related to civic affairs. I can well believe that the Mayor of the city of Detroit would need such a fund, and I am sure it is completely justifiable. One reporter wrote some years ago that slush funds are used by one venal politician to bribe another, or to seduce some unwilling virgin, and, unfortunately, many people subscribe to this view. My experience in state government would indicate that these funds are used for substantially different reasons.

It must be understood that an office holder has three kinds of expenses. First, administrative expenses—that is, payment for hotels and travel for which he is reimbursed by government. Second are political expenses—a slush fund tends to be the campaign fund in election years and there are the usual political expenses involved. Third, the office holder has personal expenses indiginous to his position in government. These may be paid out of his own pocket or, indeed, out of the slush fund but an income tax must be paid in that case. The difficulty is to distinguish political and administrative costs from personal costs.

Let me give you a sampling of my personal experiences so that you can understand the distinctions. When I first came to Lansing I had a political telephone installed both in our main Detroit office and in my Lansing office. That phone was to be used for all calls that involved politics in any way. In addition, my deputies had credit cards and their political calls were to be charged against those phone numbers. Obviously, during an election year the phone costs were substantially more than in a non-election year. I lost track of the costs of the political phones many years ago and at that time I had paid better than $100,000 out of my slush fund. Incidentally, the funding of my slush fund came from the net profits of a testimonial dinner given each year. For me and for my deputies, when a phone call was made, the question was—is it political or is it administrative? One of the more humorous incidents took place when I had several phone calls to the Keweenaw Peninsula while discussing the selection of a new branch manager in our office there. Before the business was finished the phone calls to the Keweenaw ran to more than the total amount of yearly fees paid out to the manager of the fee office. Had a civil servant made exactly the same calls and hired the same person, those calls would have been billed to the state as an administrative expense. But since my relationship to that office was that of a person picking a political appointee, I had to call it a political expense and pay for it out of the slush fund.

A second kind of political expense is sending out Christmas Cards. For some office holders this entails from 25,000 to 40,000 cards, and becomes very costly. In addition to that, most governors, for example, give out Christmas presents to a fairly limited number but in total they are also costly. This, too, must come out of a political fund and in this case it is the slush fund.

Let us consider administrative expenses. They are the easiest to arrive at because they deal directly with the administration of the office involved. For me, this would be meals, travel and hotel expenses when I am carrying out exclusively state business. I would be reimbursed by the State of Michigan for whatever those expenses were. However, all too often office holders, including myself, when traveling, are involved in both political and administrative business. There is the can of worms. How to differentiate where the costs should be allocated. Because I had a substantial patronage organization, many times I found that no matter what the trip would be, I was involved both in politics and administration. Whenever there was any question, I paid for that trip and the expenses of my deputies out of the slush fund, even though ninety percent of the trip might be involved with pure administrative detail. I remember one trip in which two of my deputies accompanied me to Escanaba. The prime reason for meeting with the branch managers in the Upper Peninsula was to discuss certain new laws that were soon going into effect concerning the sale of license plates. Unfortunately, at the end of that meeting one of the branch managers asked a political question which I had to answer. That immediately made it a political meeting and the cost of the trip became a political cost and not an administrative cost.

Now let us consider the third category—the personal costs indiginous to an office holder. In 1968, a good example developed for me. I made a trip to Washington, D.C. to participate as a member of the U.S. Highway Safety Advisory Commission. That trip turned out to be a disaster for me because the plane, instead of getting to Washington at 8 P.M., was delayed by storm until 1 A.M. Consequently, my hotel reservation had been cancelled because I was late, and I did not get to bed until 4 A.M. the next morning. I awoke at 7 A.M. and participated in a nine hour commission meeting, and finally got to bed around midnight. About 2 A.M. that morning, I suffered a heart attack. Fortunately, I was able to call the room clerk and a doctor was summoned. I was taken to the George Washington University Hospital and stayed for three weeks, and was at home for another three weeks before I could return to the office. The experience of having my second heart attack alone, in a hotel room, in a strange city, made me resolve that never again would I travel without a member of my family. This, of course, became a personal expense that could not be charged to the administration of the office. Thereafter, I paid for my wife's travel expenses out of the slush fund. I also paid income tax on the amount of money which her travel necessitated.

A second example of a personal expense was due to the fact that I was a member of the Michigan Week Commission and my particular job was to publicize and advocate the use of the Michigan State Flag. Because of this position, I was the recipient of many requests from servicemen in Vietnam who wanted a free Michigan flag. I attempted to do exactly that, and personally fulfilled each request. I received many warm letters of thanks from the servicemen, but since this was a non-political expenditure, and certainly not an administrative expenditure, it had to be paid for out of the slush fund. Here again, I paid a personal income tax on the amount of money spent for the flags —about two hundred of them over a period of three years. I was delighted when General Abrams ordered servicemen to cease flying state flags in Vietnam because of the severe competition that was aroused between the states.

Another interesting example of the cost of holding public office was "Mission Michigan." This expedition was organized by supporters of Governor Romney in 1965 and the intent was to have a trade mission go to six countries in western Europe with the hope of increasing trade between the State of Michigan and those countries. Approximately fifty businessmen took part in the trip as well as eight legislators, divided evenly between Democrats and Republicans, Governor Romney and myself. The trip took ten days and was a flying tour of Holland, Germany, Italy, France, Switzerland and England. Upon returning, I had to make the decision as to whether the trip was political, administrative or personal. The legislators in both the Senate and House had voted themselves an appropriation to pay their expenses. The businessmen paid their own expenses. The Governor, as the leader of the trip, got a free ride. I decided the trip was not advantageous to me politically, so it could not be a political charge, and the Secretary of State's office had nothing to do with foreign trade, therefore it could not be an administrative cost. That left nothing but a personal cost for me and I took the $1100 out of the slush fund.

One of the best examples of what can happen was the experience of former Mayor Louis Miriani of Detroit, who took monies from his private fund and made private investments for himself. The federal Internal Revenue office thought that he should have paid an income tax on that money. He argued that it was a free-will gift and the people who donated the money to the fund through testimonial dinners agreed with him. But that did not satisfy the income tax people and, as a result, Louis Miriani is now serving a prison sentence for income tax evasion.

I believe that one of the defects of this system is that it depends on what office you hold and who you are. A president or governor can take his wife on a trip, which is at least partly political in nature, and no one is concerned when the cost of the trip is paid for by either the federal or state government. But if a township supervisor or a councilman in a local town attempted the same thing he would find that his wife's passage would not be paid for by local government.

A second defect is that many trips and expenses are both administrative and political in nature. The office holder has to allow his conscience to make the decision whether to pay for them out of a private fund or to bill the state for the cost of the trip. Since I had to administer what some of the newspapers called a "patronage empire" almost everything I did had a political tinge. As a result, I was almost unable to bill the state for expenses and over a long period of years I averaged less than twenty dollars a month in reimbursements from the state.

Small wonder that office holders are very reluctant to talk about their private funds or that the press zealously attempts to find out not only how the money for the fund is raised, but how it is spent.

VIII

THE NEWS MEDIA

I have acquired a new respect for the news media since writing this book. I find it difficult to obtain the skill required to put together a readable and coherent exposition, although I have no time limit or deadline to work against. The skills of the newspaperman draw my strongest admiration. On three occasions during my public career I attended meetings at which I had little comprehension of what was going on. I was unable to understand the motivation of the speakers or, indeed, to sort out their recommendations and objectives. Usually these meetings were chaotic without a strong presiding officer, and the speakers continually interrupted each other. After reading the news reports of these three meetings, I was amazed at the clarity and understanding which the reporters who covered the meetings were able to convey to their readers. I have not only admiration but some envy for their profession.

During my tenure in office, certain changes took place in the functioning of the Capitol Press Corps. Some I quite agreed with but had latent doubts about others. I approved of the introduction of women into the pressroom. Only in the last several years have women appeared there as reporters. I found that they were really more perceptive than men in the human qualities of politics, and often gave more balance to their reports by interpreting both the man and the issue. On the other hand the Capitol Press Corps had one change that I did not like at all. Reporters from the news agencies and the big metropolitan papers were being changed very often. Apparently their editors wanted novice reporters to have experience in many fields. Thus, they would only keep them in the Capitol News Bureau office for a year or two and then transfer them to another assignment. No doubt it was favorable in terms of experience for the new reporter, but unfavorable for the politician involved, since a new reporter appearing from time to time had to be reeducated. They had little background on many issues and, more importantly, they lacked the personal news sources which a long time veteran acquires.

The manner in which the reporter or television man set up the stories could make or break a politician's efforts on a particular issue or, indeed, his political career. Just the choice of words would make a world of difference. For instance, if the reporter wrote that a politician *revealed* or *admitted* something, the inference was that it was bad. On the other hand, if the reporter was simply *told* something, there was no connotation of goodness or badness. One reporter I shall never forget was Owen Deatrick of the *Detroit Free Press,* for the in-depth study he did on Governor Kim Sigler. From time to time he would write a story in which the sentences would read, "and Governor Sigler, before coming to work with one of his 47 suits"; or it would be reported as "Kim Sigler this morning selected a bright blue pattern from his closet full of clothes." The inference of course was that Sigler was a clothes horse and it certainly did him no good by the time he came up for re-election against G. Mennen Williams.

During my entire sixteen years as Secretary of State, the one item that kept recurring was the question of whether the branch managers who sell license plates should be under Civil Service or should be my personal appointees. Sometimes the reporter appeared to have strong and emotional feelings on this subject, and I could always recognize his personal feelings by the manner in which the story was written. If the reporter came forth with a statement that the issue was the spoils system versus the Civil Service system, I knew that he was an advocate of the Civil Service side. However, if he talked about salaried offices versus fee offices, then I thought it was straight reporting, although I may have been prejudiced.

On one occasion I was trapped by a reporter and I shall not soon forget him. This reporter, without telling me that he was writing an expose on the Legislature, called me about twice a week for four weeks and chatted on innocuous subjects, but he would use, what I later learned, were loaded questions. For example, he would say "The parties the legislators are having are lasting longer and more liquor is being served than usual. Don't they have a high old time?" My reply was "Could be, guess so." Or when he talked about the slow progress of legislation moving through the Senate and gave the opinion that they were not working as hard as they might, I did not disagree. On a third occasion he talked about the salaries of the Michigan legislators and I verified the fact that the members were paid as well or better than a majority in other states. The net result of this was an article quoting James Hare as saying that the Legislature was one of the worst examples of governmental bureaucracy that he had ever witnessed, and the legislators were lazy, slow, drunkards, overpaid, indifferent and worthless. It was useless to issue a denial or rebuttal. It would have only made it worse. The fact was that everything he wrote was a reasonable, factual interpretation of my statements, but when combined, they became a vitriolic blast against each and all of the legislators, which, of course, I never would have said on my own.

In an election year, one of the things to watch was to see if a particular reporter was bucking for a job with one of the candidates in Washington or Lansing, or with the State Central Committee of one of the policial parties. I could almost sense when that was taking place, because all of a sudden the reporter's or news commentator's discourse about a candidate would become favorable, not in outright terms but in the kinds of adjectives he used to describe the candidate or his opponent. If a candidate was described as diligent, hard-working, intelligent, determined, resourceful and had a lovely family, I always wondered whether some reporter was going to become a political press secretary after the election. I remember being with friends one evening and going through the press clips of reporters who had been on a campaign trail with us. Two of the reporters had become aides in the political offices of men whom they had covered during the campaign period. And to those of us reading the press clips there was never any question that the reporters during the campaign period had made a diligent effort to build up a particular candidate.

On the other hand, there were reporters whom I considered to be straight writers and there was one characteristic about them which appeared in their newspaper stories—they used practically no adjectives in their narratives. They made no connotations or inferences of right or wrong. It was strictly straight reporting of what the candidate or his opponent said and did. I always admired that. The reporters whom I personally evaluated as reasonable and fair were those who attempted to get both sides of every story in the *same* issue of the paper. For example, one candidate might blast his opponent and if a reporter wanted a sensational story he could print just that statement, then the next day, follow-up by printing the opponents side of the argument. Unfortunately, the rebuttal on the second day might well appear on page seventeen while the original attack appeared on page one.

When good reporters did not fully understand a press release, they would immediately call the issuing politico and get a further refinement or clarification. The highest honor that any reporter could give to a political office holder would be to get the story from him and, after writing it, check back with the office holder to find if the quotes were correct.

Two men in the reportorial corps stand out in my memory as outstanding reporters with whom I had worked for almost twenty years. One was Carl Rudow, now retired, but then at the *Detroit News,* and Bill Baird of the *Lansing State Journal* who is still reporting. Unfortunately, good, straight reporting does not always make the best headlines. The story that is one-sided, vitriolic and violent in nature tends to appear in fiery headlines and sell newspapers. I believe I am paying the highest tribute possible to the news media in this book simply by the extensive use of quotations from the people in this profession.

IX

PUBLIC DISCLOSURE

OF all the lost causes and hopeless enterprises in which I have been involved, one that stands out in my memory is my advocacy of a law that would bring about Public Disclosure in Michigan Government.

While I have pursued it for ten years (between 1960 and 1970) I knew from the very beginning that it was a lost cause. But it was a most interesting one. I knew from the beginning that such a law was opposed by both Houses of the Michigan Legislature, to say nothing of opposition from both political parties, although no one would condemn it publicly.

A public disclosure law, as I advocated it, would have affected elected officials in Michigan Government as well as the officers of the two major parties. In essence it would have required that the person subject to the law would publicly declare both the amounts and the sources of his yearly income, as well as his net worth at the end of each year. Both Presidents Truman and Johnson had publicly endorsed the idea. When Richard Nixon and Hubert Humphrey were vying for the presidency, each made a voluntary public disclosure of their financial background. Often I was asked by citizens who were frankly puzzled, what is the need for a public disclosure law, are not all people in government relatively honest? I pointed out that when people were nominated for Supreme Court Justices of the United States, the Senate always asked each one of them for a full financial disclosure for the past years. Therefore, it does not seem unreasonable to ask it from public officials in other capacities on the state level.

The need for such a law is closely tied to the question—what is conflict of interest? I think that all persons involved or interested in government will agree that no person in public office should be in a situation where there is conflict of interest between his duties and his financial betterment. There is no other way of determining whether a governmental official is profiting through his public office unless there is some kind of document telling the public about his total income. Indeed, there is another good reason for a public disclosure law—the sources of income, even though there is nothing wrong with those sources, give a better indication of the interests of a public official than any public statement he may make on the campaign trail. Certainly if a part of his income comes privately from a union, corporation, a law firm or private investments, all of these sources tend to influence his thinking.

On the national front, gains have been made because of the financial problems of Bobby Baker and Senator Dodd. The U.S. Senate, after months of debate, decided they should bring forth a public disclosure resolution. They did this on May 22, 1968. It follows:

RULE XLIV
Disclosure of Financial Interests
1. Each Senator or person who has declared or otherwise made known his intention to seek nomination of election, or who has filed papers or petitions for nominatpon or election, or on whose behalf a declaration or nominating paper or petition has been made or filed, or who has otherwise, directly or indirectly manifested his intention to seek nomination or election, pursuant to State law, to the office of United States Senator, and, each officer or employee of the Senate who is compensated at a rate in excess of $15,000 a year, shall file with the Comptroller General of the United States, in a sealed envelope marked "Confidential Personal Financial Disclosure of   , before the 15th day of May in each year, the following reports of his personal financial interests:

    (a) a copy of the returns of taxes, declarations, statements, or other documents which he, or he and his spouse jointly, made for the preceding year in compliance with the income tax provisions of the Internal Revenue Code:

(b) the amount or value and source of each fee or compensation or $1,000 or more received by him during the preceding year from a client; and

(c) the name and address of each business or professional corporation, firm or enterprise in which he was an officer, director, partner, proprietor, or employee who received compensation during the preceding year and the amount of such compensation;

(d) the identity of each interest in real or personal property having a value of $10,000 or more which he owned at any time during the preceding year;

(e) the identity of each trust or other fiduciary relation in which he held a beneficial interest having a value of $10,000 or more, and the identity if known of each interest of the trust or other fiduciary relation in real or personal property in which the Senator, officer, or employee held a beneficial interest having a value of $10,000 or more at any time during the preceding year. If he cannot obtain the identity of the fiduciary interests, the Senator, officer, or employee shall request the fiduciary to report that information to the Comptroller General in the same manner that reports are filed under this rule;

(f) the identity of each liability of $5,000 or more owed by him, or by him and his spouse jointly, at any time during the preceding year; and

(g) the source and value of all gifts in the aggregate amount of value of $50 or more from any single source received by him during the preceding year.

Section I of Rule XLIV was deceiving. It was like the old gag describing the insurance policy; what the company gave the beneficiary in the large print, it took away in the small print. In this case, Section II of Rule XLIV was the small print, and it almost completely nullified SectionI. In Section II, it provided that the sealed financial record of any Senator should be kept by the Comptroller General and remain sealed. Only a majority of the ethics committee of the Senate could bring it before that body and, even then, the financial record would not be made available to the press or the general public. Also, in the event of the retirement or death of any Senator, the sealed documents were to be returned to him or to his estate.

The net result was that instead of being a public disclosure document it was in reality a private concealment document with the full agreement of the Senate.

In my pursuit of a new law, I talked informally with many members of both the House and Senate, and the leaders of the two political parties. I found that about one-fourth of the members of the House and one-third of the members of the Senate had no real opposition to a public disclosure law. The leaders of the Democratic Party did not wish to talk about the subject. Even those who had no opposition also had no willingness to take a leadership position because no one wanted to become involved in the personal recriminations that would take place. Those who opposed such a law were in vehement opposition. The first argument, of course, was that it was an invasion of privacy. I pointed out to them that a public official is hardly in the same position as a private citizen, and that his life and financial transactions are not protected by the same provisions. During these several years, the machinations of Bobby Baker in Washington certainly helped my cause. Within the last two years the most peculiar situation concerning the Secretary of State of Illinois, who died and left an alleged two million dollars in shoe boxes in his closet, gave pause for consideration on the part of those people who opposed such a law.

Some of the politicians in opposition, I thought, had really quite reasonable arguments. One man said he was ashamed to admit he had no income other than his salary in the Legislature. Two others did not want to expose the fact that they were financially dependent upon their wives. Another told me in all frankness that he would be willing to give me the name, address and telephone number of his mistress, but he would never give a financial disclosure statement. One Senator pointed out that he had a law retainer annual fee from a corporation that had substantial interest in legislation pending in the Senate, and argued that while he had voted against supporting the interests of that particular corporation, he would be exposed to criticism for having the account.

Several of the legislators questioned me as to how they could personally make a public disclosure statement, but wondered where they would file it. I had to admit that since there was no law on the subject, all they could do would be to file it with some official such as myself or the Governor, and give a copy of it to the press. Many of them demurred because they feared it would make them appear to be "holier than thou." Of course, one of the defects of having individuals make their own separate disclosure statement was that there was no specific form the statement should take, and no two of them would be alike.

There were persons who did make the effort in spite of the problems of not knowing how or with whom to file a report. One of the most interesting of these was a report filed by Theodore Souris when he was a Supreme Court Justice. In October of 1967, while he was contemplating running for re-election as Justice, a testimonial dinner was given. That dinner took in a gross figure of about $24,000. By 1968, he decided he was not going to be a candidate for re-election and the question was how to account for the monies raised. His solution was to refund to the contributors of that dinner a pro-rata figure to all those who desired a refund, and give the remainder of the money, $12,000, to two charitable social agencies in Wayne County. This very detailed and meticulous report was filed in my office with instructions that it was available to the press or anyone interested.

Another regular filer of financial statements for many years was Emil Lockwood, leader of the Republicans in the Senate. He yearly filed, with my office and the Governor's office, a detailed statement of profit and loss as well as net worth at the end of each year. I myself filed a copy of my income tax report with the Chairman of the House Policy Committee in the House of Representatives and also with the Director of Elections. It was hardly a popular position to take and admittedly a lost cause from my standpoint. Chief Justice Thomas Brennan of the Supreme Court also filed a report.

To conclude, I think the statement of Jesse Unruh who is Mr. Democrat of California is interesting. He has held office there longer than any man I know. He had this to say about legislative ethics and conflict of interest, specifically on full disclosure.

There is an old saying that there are no secrets in politics. Like most other simplistic sayings it is not always true in every case but it could be. If some enterprising reporter or an aggressive opponent desires to dig deep enough and hard enough he can usually find out the best hidden of information. The danger lies in the fact that if this is the way the information is derived it will be presented as the total picture.

That fact plus others have led me to believe strongly in full disclosure of holdings income, and campaign contributions. Far better that all of the facts are laid bare than to rely upon your opposition or the press to divulge part of them.

I think also the legislative branch is most in need of repairing public confidence in it and while full disclosure may not materially affect the probity of the legislative branch it will seem to do so with the general public—which, as Machiavelli said, may be more important. Particularly is this necessary now as we move to increase the capacity of the legislative branch. As cases of individual cupidity are exposed in the Legislature (and I think this will continue at some level at least) there is little defense for the Legislature as an institution. If full disclosure was operative this would provide some line of institutional defense. Disclosure should of course apply to challengers for office as well as incumbents. The two or three states which have moved in this field have not proven anything very permanently yet except that the system still works despite some discomfort to a few individuals.

A statute forbidding a legislator (or judge or executive) from engaging in activities which constitute a major conflict is also desirable—largely for the same reason—inspiring more public confidence.

Beyond this, I have a few other things to add in the way of general approaches. I am convinced that proper decision-making tools are perhaps more valuable in avoiding conflicts than almost any legislation. William Pincus of the Ford Foundation states accurately that most corruption occurs because only a very few are privy to a situation wherein it occurs. Add a few bright young staff people to a committee, he says, and the chances of apprehension of the wrongdoers are enhanced.

Ambition and visibility are also major deterrents to the kind of old-fashioned vote buying that Jay Gould boasted of in the late nineteenth century. The politician who is looking for support for his next step is far less likely to be involved in personal financial dishonesty than his stagnating colleague.

The general approach, however, is much more difficult to resolve. By general I mean the approach that we all, or each of us, take to resolving conflicts.

I feel strongly that there is no single answer for everyone in every situation. The final answer will again usually be a variation of Machiavelli's theme. Is the officeholder credible to the public? The other, less obvious answer is whether he can live with himself.

During my career I have served as Speaker, chairman of the Appropriations Committee, chairman of the Finance and Insurance Committee and now as Minority Leader. I have also managed two gubernatorial campaigns, a presidential campaign, several presidential primaries, acted as chief fund raiser for legislative Democrats, and gotten myself re-elected seven times. I doubt that I have hewed to a constant line in just my own thinking much less my actions.

I have not become so antiseptic that I have not made money on outside ventures or activities. Conversely I have tried to confine moneymaking to activities which may have occurred because of my office but not by use of my office—a subtle distinction perhaps but an important one. In a part-time Legislature particularly, I do not think we can expect our legislators to forswear every opportunity for personal gain. What we should expect is that they not use their office for that.

This I do not suggest is the perfect answer, but until we are willing to pay directly the costs of government; until our salaries, pensions and working conditions are far beyond what they are now and until the people are willing to preperly and directly finance campaigns I suggest it is the best we can do.

Your success will be largely like the success of our monetary system—only as good as the people believe it is.

A story in the *Detroit Free Press* of April 20, 1971, illustrated better than anything I can say the essence of politics, and also the abhorrence that both public officials and party officers feel about a public disclosure.

DEM FUND'S SOURCE TO REMAIN SECRET

The treasurer of Michigan's Democratic party says it is none of the public's business where the party gets its money for day-to-day political operations.

But most of this money comes from sources other than organized labor, insists treasurer Stuart E. Hertzberg.

He refused, however, to disclose party financial records—kept in his downtown Detroit law office—showing who contributed to a $225,000 fund that he said the party spent but did not report publicly in 1970.

The only public record of 1970 income and spending by the party was filed in the clerk's office of Oakland County, where Hertzberg resides.

That report shows the Michigan Democratic Party received $78,420.94, spent $90,365.14, and had debts of $10,873.14 during the 1970 general election.

Of the $78,420.94 listed as income, the report showed the U A W contributed $30,343.82 and at least $1,620 came from other unions.

Based on the contents of that report, one of a series of stories about Michigan campaign financing in the Free Press last week concluded that labor contributed a major share of the day-to-day operations of the party.

Sam Fishman, the U A W's liaison man with Michigan politics and one of the Democrats' more influential figures, protested that such a conclusion exaggerated labor's role in financing Democratic operations.

The State central committee spent at least a quarter of a million dollars in 1970, Fishman said, adding that labor's proportionate contribution was not nearly as great as that suggested by the party report filed in Oakland County. He referred a reporter to Hertzberg to obtain actual figures.

Of the conclusion that labor contributed a major share to the party's day-to-day operation, Hertzberg declared: 'That's a 100 percent falsehood.'

He said the $78,420.94 that he reported on the Oakland County records reflects only money the party received from Aug. 3 to Nov. 3, 1970.

'Besides, the $78,420.94 that was reported,' Hertzberg said, 'the party spent an additional $225,000 or more during 1970.' 'Only a small amount of the unreported $225,000 was contributed by labor,' he said.

A Free Press reporter asked to see the party financial records in Hertzberg's office to determine who contributed the money.

Hertzberg said: 'I don't think any useful purpose would be served for me to show you who contributed.'

'I had a President's Club (for then President Lyndon B. Johnson) in 1964. It was a national club. It was $1,000 a year (for membership). The Detroit newspapers wrote a story about it and made it look dirty, and I refuse to give out the names (of party contributors) now.'

'If somebody gives $1,000, I see nothing wrong. If a guy gives $1,000 why should it sound dirty?' Further Hertzberg said, 'There are some people in business in Michigan who wouldn't want other business people to know what they gave.'

He explained that if it were disclosed that some vendors to big corporations contributed to the Democrats' $100 or $500 clubs, the vendors' business might be hurt.

Hertzberg said the party complies with an accepted interpretation of Michigan's law regulating political spending. He said the law requires a disclosure of party funds received and spent only during the general election of a campaign year.

Under that interpretation of the law, the party will make no public report on the money contributed to meet a $266,590 budget for 1971.

The Republican Party also follows the interpretation of the law that party finances must be reported only during general elections.

In 1970, the Republican State Central Committee reported it received $457,977.87 in contributions between Aug. 4 to Nov. 3.

The Republican Party's budget for 1971 totals $2.1 million, of which more than $700,000 is to pay off back campaign debts and $420,000 will be sent to the national GOP for election purposes. None of that will be reported if the customary interpretation of the disclosure law is followed.

A spokesman in Attorney General Frank J. Kelley's office said the law requiring disclosure of political spending by political parties during non-election years and during primary elections 'can be argued either way' and is viewed, as are most other sections of the law, to be unenforceable.

Hertzberg was asked if he felt no obligation to disclose party finances, even if the law doesn't require it, since the Democratic Party is a public body.

He replied: 'When the state laws require it, we'll comply 100 percent with state laws. The state laws don't require in a non-campaign year that we disclose our contributors.'

'Anybody who is active in politics has a pretty good idea where the money comes from, in campaign years, and non-campaign years. I'd think a person would be pretty naive if he didn't know where the money comes from. There have been newspaper articles about it.'

Hertzberg said in election years labor does contribute 'substantially to campaigns.'

Incidentially, I might say that in the years 1955 to 1960, which were the first six years of my administration and the last six years of Governor Williams' administration, the Democratic State Central Committee did file a detailed report of all expenditures and receipts with the Director of Elections, which were open to public scrutiny. Once the Democrats had lost the Governorship, it became the decision of the Democratic State Central Committee whether to continue filing these reports. They decided strongly against it.

X

PRIVACY OR CONCEALMENT

THERE is a bit of flap going on these days among public officials who object to an "invasion of their privacy." One congressman, in fact, has denounced the FBI for bugging his office and wiretapping his telephone. On the other hand, the law enforcement authorities are asking for new laws that will permit them to wiretap telephones in the investigation of criminal offenses. The question becomes how great is the right to privacy and for whom? I think privacy must be defined as being different from secrecy or concealment and a decision must be made as to whether or not public officials should have the same right to privacy that a private citizen should have. In the late 1950's I was informed, on two different occasions, that some unknown person had tapped my telephone lines. The telephone linemen explained that one of the taps was at a pole some distance from the Capitol and one of them right in the switchboard in our own office. After some thought I concluded—what difference would it make? About the only real enjoyment anyone might get out of my conversations would be my comments on how the Detroit Tigers were doing.

A public official should have less protection under the moral question of personal privacy than a private citizen could expect. But it is a very fine line as to how much privacy the politician or the office holder should expect. Let me give you some examples. Certainly, the police and the law enforcement officials must have the maximum privacy when conducting criminal investigations. To permit outsiders to legally wiretap police lines would make a farce out of law enforcement. Yet, the need for permitting the police to wiretap when confronted with the power of organized crime becomes more reasonable. I have recited, in previous chapters, my difficulty in attempting to get public officials to make public disclosure of their sources and amounts of income. This is a most unpopular issue with most public officials. They usually argue that it is a violation of their personal privacy and, so far, they have made that argument stick.

I am not too concerned that the use of the privacy dodge is going to allow too much skullduggery or embezzlement of public funds or tax dodging, but rather that privacy or more truly concealment of facts is a very dangerous situation. Public policy relies on the personal judgment of people in government and those personal judgments should be made by knowing all the facts surrounding a particular situation. If some of the facts are withheld, the judgments are faulty and the policies are worse. Personally, I wonder how much of the difficulty that our country has in Vietnam is due to faulty policies based on bad judgments founded on a lack of factual information.

One of the interesting examples of concealing facts was the push in the mid-1950's to remove racial designation from all employment applications and records in state government. No one had any real objection to this and it was done rather forthrightly during Governor Williams' administration. Later, in the 1970's, a new and different judgment had to be made—what percentage of the persons employed by the state government belong to minority groups and what percentage of them secured promotions and were in the higher echelon. With race removed as a designation from all records, there was nothing to rely on and a headcount had to be taken in all the departments of state government to secure the necessary information.But the original decision to remove the racial designation had been made because it was an invasion of personal privacy and not meaningful to the employment record.

Another example turned up in the early 1960's. A question was raised regarding university faculties and whether or not too many of the professors were spending too much time acting as consultants to private business and not giving adequate supervision to their classes.

Rumor had it that some $20,000 a year faculty members were earning another $20,000 as private consultants. When the reporters descended upon the campuses to find out what the salaries were, they were told this was a matter of personal privacy and would not be disclosed.

In many states the law controlling lobbyists demands that the lobbyist make a report semi-anually to the Legislature stating their expenses in lobbying. In this state, any efforts in the direction of requiring such reports have been met with the rhetoric, "That is an invasion of personal privacy." To this date, lobbyists have made that one stick.

There are certain areas in which the government functions, where there seems to be no argument against allowing complete privacy or, indeed, concealment. In the public health records, the records on delayed marriages and illegitimate births are considered sacrosanct and are not released to anyone other than the person named in the record. A new facet entering the picture on the privacy front is the more extensive use of computers as record-keepers. By the end of the 1970's, every department of state government, I suspect, will have all its records computerized. This means that an all-points bulletin going out from a police investigation office would get complete information about individuals which would be of help to the law enforcement authorities. For example, an all-points bulletin asking for all information on John Doe might get a return about his educational record, mental health record, driving record, police criminal record, occupational record as to whether he was licensed in a craft or profession, his record with the social welfare division, credit record and marital experience. This is nothing new, except that at the present time if the police asked for the same type of record it would involve either individual trips or letters to many different offices. Today, the manpower required precludes an extensive use of the records, but once the computers are used, a request for total information on an individual could be answered in a matter of minutes. The concept of privacy certainly shrinks. My opinion is that a public official, once he takes office, loses his right to privacy. When he is on the public payroll and spending or receiving public tax monies, I think his duty is to forego his right of privacy and disclose any requested information.

There is a subtle form of concealment, unrecognized by the public, which flourishes among public administrators. The administrator refuses to reveal what standards and what quality he demands for productivity and successful operation within his jurisdiction. In other words, it is very difficult to say whether any program within a state department is successful or unsuccessful in comparison with the same departments in other states. Some administrators, of course, set no standards and, thus, have nothing to conceal. They also have nebulous goals which are too difficult to pin down.

I faced this problem early in my administration when I attempted to evaluate the success or failure of traffic safety programs in Michigan. Fortunately, we had two reliable statistics from which to form judgments and make standards. These two statistics were the number of deaths in a certain area during a particular time period and, secondly, the amount of gasoline used in the same period in the same area, so that a judgment could be made about the number of deaths per hundred million miles driven by all motorists in a particular jurisdiction. Our standards and goals became the attempt to hold the number of deaths per hundred million miles driven to less than four. We were never able to achieve this on a state-wide basis, but some counties and many cities made a very creditable showing by this standard. Michigan's death rate of from four to five deaths per hundred million miles placed us in the mid-group of all the states in the country and gave us a great deal of room for improvement. But at least we knew what was possible and could look to the states that had better records and attempt to learn what could be done to improve our record.

Unfortunately, not all departments of state government have standards of the kind that can be reduced to figures. They are all too often only pious hopes and not hard and fast statistical standards. As an old schoolteacher, I have always been interested in what is a good school or a good school district, and have learned all the pitfalls of trying to judge standards or make judgments. The facts are, I am afraid, that one cannot say that the fourth grade in school A is better or worse than the fourth grade in school B; or that high school X in Center City is better than high school Y in Central Valley. I have heard many parents contend that a particular school was superior with great enrichment for the pupils. I never knew exactly what that meant, but I often thought it meant that the superintendent in that school district had a good public relations program going for him. Another argument against trying to measure success or failure in the educational business is that many of the goals are indefinable, such as happy students, satisfied faculty, students eager to learn, emotional stability among the student body and other factors that cannot be counted or tabulated.

When school teachers are pushing for a raise, they are able to tabulate very well. They know the comparative salary structures of every school district in the state and can enumerate the dollar costs of the fringe benefits to be found everywhere. I have a suspicion that you can always find the standards and comparisons if you really want to. It is possible, in the exact sciences, to determine whether a student is learning a particular amount of tangible information. In the language field the proficiency of a student can be measured. There are, of course, difficulties in the social sciences in measuring how much a student learns, appreciates or carries over into his daily life, but again there are certain factual measurements that can be made. In the health education field they revel in statistics. The runner, swimmer, high jumper or the pole vaulter can determine to a fraction of an inch, or second, how successful they are. Certainly the football scores are memorized by thousands of people.

It is my feeling that the educational system could put forth some hard and fast standards that would allow for measurements of intellectual success by the schools, school districts or between the states. I realize the great difficulties in achieving formulation of a standard, but also have a terrible suspicion that some of the administrators involved want no part of submitting standards easily interpreted by the public. This most subtle form of concealment is not good for the system, the students or the public.

If they tell you that they do have standards, ask for a list of the ten best schools and the ten worst schools in the state.

I have talked exclusively about schools because tremendous amounts of money have been poured into this area of government. The same question of goals, standards and results can be applied to any part of state government. When you hear there are no standards then you have good cause to be suspicious. If they do have standards then they can make comparisons between one jurisdiction and another. In short, concealment hides the facts that judgments have to be based on, and without them you can have no rational public policy.

XI

ECONOMY AND EFFICIENCY

I have never known a politician on the campaign trail who was not in favor of economy and efficiency in government, at least until he got back to Lansing or Washington. These two words are *image* words and like other terms such as Civil Service, spoils system, patronage, slush funds or charisma, they have different meanings to different people. To one man efficiency and economy would mean reducing governmental costs, reducing his own tax burden. Many retirees fall into this classification. This man, of course, votes against increases in school millage elections and on the local government level opposes all tax increases. He feels that he can do something about his tax burden on the local level. I wonder how many of them know that of all the tax dollars, probably eighty-three or eighty-four percent of the total monies collected, go to the Federal Government and that the county, city, township and the schools, together with the state, divide the remaining sixteen or seventeen percent of these taxes.

Another man thinks of efficiency in government as having governmental clerks working hard at their desks and being responsive to the questions which citizens may ask them.

Words such as efficiency and economy, Civil Service, social welfare and educational enrichment have a favorable connotation; while other words such as spoils system, slush funds, patronage and government hacks have an opposite reaction. Sometimes the good words are in competition with each other rather than opposing the bad words.

For example, I can go back to my theme of a patronage system for selling license plates being twice as economical as a Civil Service system. But, on the other hand, it would be inefficient to use a patronage system in hiring engineers for the Highway Department. All too often the average citizen thinks of efficiency as another term for better service for his own particular needs.

Over the years I have had many requests, usually by mail, asking that license plates be ordered and sold through the mail. The argument in favor was always to the effect that it would be a more efficient governmental service. In reality it would be a more convenient service for license plate buyers. I have always rejected the thought of mail service for license plates because in the few states where it does operate, the costs of the total operation skyrocket, and with the new mailing rates the costs of providing plates by that method would probably double. I have never felt that the state had to provide special service for the car owner, when it only demanded a single trip to the branch office once a year. Certainly that same customer goes to the store far more often and does not demand mail service from his grocer.

About eight or nine years ago, the state instituted a survey of governmental departments and agencies to determine which ones were efficient or less than efficient, and the method used was to set a time standard for certain kinds of operations. It so happened that one of the subdivisions of the Secretary of State's office was selected to be a testee in the survey. The results were very gratifying and I publicly submitted it for approval. What was being measured was the speed and quality control of filing names and cards and interpreting them in the drivers license files, and the division being tested came out with almost a ninety-nine percent efficiency rating. Later we began to substitute the use of computers for manual files in the drivers license area. Since there are more than five million drivers and some of them with very extensive records, the computer fitted our needs very nicely and was much faster, both to file into and, even more importantly, to get the information out of almost instantly. It has been mathematically proven that the methods which rated highly as a manual operation were only one-twentieth as efficient as a computer.

However, neither of these standards and measurements are relevant. The important thing in bringing about true economy is how well a computer will operate in helping the State Department reach its goal of improving the traffic safety record of the state. It makes no difference how fast or efficiently the records are processed. The only thing that really counts is whether or not the number of accidents on the highways can be reduced. It is only when you measure the fulfillment of a goal within a governmental department that you can truly give it a rating.

An even better example of a goal in determining a governmental efficiency rating occurred at a Senate appropriations hearing back in the early 1960's. A sixty-five year old woman was testifying before the Senate Committee and making an emotional plea for more welfare funds. Her story was that as a young caseworker, forty years earlier, she worked with a young man and wife who had four children. These four children married and three out of the four families also became a part of the welfare case load. Then this good woman, who is now a supervisor in the Welfare Department, said "those four families now have produced twelve children and seven of them are now on the welfare rolls." She thought that this was a magnificent argument in favor of more welfare funds. Her concept of her job was to provide food, shelter and security for the needy. She did not think her job was to put these people back into the working world, and indeed it was not her job, so that it was a question of whether her efficiency in securing the funds and distributing them was the proper goal.

All too often, the headlines record a victory for a group when the Legislature approves new millions of dollars to a particular project. Certainly this is not a victory for economy, but if the goal in mind is a worthwhile one and the money appropriated gets good social results, then it can be called efficiency. The money being poured into social welfare and education in this state needs to be studied in terms of what the ultimate goals are, whether the recipients of the welfare are being moved back into the working world, and whether the students are receiving worthwhile enrichment.

One small agency which I dealt with over the entire sixteen years as Secretary of State was the Michigan Traffic Safety Commission. This agency had from three to seven members on its staff, depending on the year and the availability of money. Its duty in life was to coordinate the traffic safety activities of several of the larger departments of state government: the Governor's office, the State Police, the Secretary of State's office, the Highway Commission and the Superintendent of Public Instruction. The executive secretary of the agency was Gerald Shipman who had previously been the Director of a Traffic Safety Council in Benton Harbor and who knew the value of getting voluntary help in any situation. He worked long and hard in an effort to establish new traffic safety councils throughout the state and was reasonably successful in view of his exceedingly small budget. He did this by taking trips outstate and encouraging the formation of new safety councils in the larger towns, as well as coordinating the efforts of those already established. More importantly, he was enlisting the private citizen in an effort that was not primarily governmental. The state could have taken an entirely different tact and subsidized numerous traffic safety offices in twenty cities and towns using civil servants to do exactly the same jobs which volunteer traffic safety councils were doing. My admiration for Shipman was not only for the job he did, but because he utilized private citizens in a voluntary capacity at a very substantial saving to the state.

The State Safety Commission met once a month at the State Capitol, and was extremely well attended by the representatives of forty other organizations. The various state departments, such as the State Police and my own department, made reports. When further action was recommended, these representatives went back to their counties and tried to get the action underway. Three of the representatives stand out in my mind. They faithfully attended each meeting, year after year, and then went back to their home counties and beleaguered the police and court officials to put more power into the traffic safety programs. The three were Mrs. Ann Harmon from Howell in Livingston County, Mrs. Mildred Dunbar from Mt. Pleasant in Isabella

County and Mrs. Jo Whetzel from Royal Oak in Oakland County. The determination and enthusiasm of these women proved very effective in getting results.

In an effort to achieve both economy and efficiency in government, care must be taken that the long range goals are not completely the product of good intentions. In the 1930's, when Molotov was the Chairman of the Council of People's Commissars of Russia, he made a most cynical yet true observation, that the U.S. Public Health Service and the Rockefeller Foundation were the best friends of long-range communism in Latin America. He meant that the efforts of these two fine institutions to raise the birth rate and lower the death rate in the Latin American countries, without sufficient food production, would expand the number of people living in poverty. Americans are idealistic and often think that good intentions plus large appropriations add up to make a better world. All too often the long range goals correct one social evil but may very well build up a greater one.

Quite often a public official has to make a very personal decision as to whether he will practice economy when it affects himself or his own individual office. The State Constitution states: "the legislature shall provide that the salary of any state officer, while acting as governor, shall be equal to that of the governor." In my sixteen years as Secretary of State, I performed as the Acting Governor for two hundred days. The question became, should I ask for the Governor's salary during the period in which I was the Acting Governor? After giving it some thought I decided that the additional duties—signing a few legislative bills, presiding over meetings which I would have to attend anyway, or filling in for the Governor when irate citizens had a protest—were not sufficiently onerous for me to receive the Governor's pay check for that period.

There is a much quoted saying that government should only do for the people the things they cannot do for themselves. Unfortunately, due to its complexities, the people are calling more and more on the government to do things which they used to do for themselves.

Let me relate a story of how a cooperative community working together with private enterprise was spurred on by a resolute and determined individual to perform an impossible task. This is the story of Long Lake in Oakland County, a lake suffering from serious eutrophication. It was filling with silt and reeds, and swamp plants were appearing everywhere; a scum of algae formed around the edges. I had a most personal interest in this project because I had a cottage on the south shore and had watched the lake over a period of ten years degenerate from a thing of beauty to a semi-swamp. The homeowners around the lake had seen their property values cut in half over a very short period of time.

Because of my own private concern, I made a trip to the State Department of Conservation to get their advice on what to do with a dying lake. The answer I got was that it is an almost irreversible trend and that in Michigan there were literally hundreds of lakes going through the same process. They told me I could expect no help from the government since the reversal of the trend in any lake was a most expensive process, and it was impossible for the state to provide this expensive rehabilitation. They recommended to me that I meet and talk with an individual who was extremely interested in the possibility of reclaiming and rehabilitating dying lakes. This man was a Lansing resident, Donald Rutter, who listened to my description of this lake without batting an eye. I explained to him that the experts in ecology to whom I had talked believed it to be an irreversible trend in the development of the lake. I explained there were no monies available to even begin taking a survey; there were no tax powers within that township which could levy an equitable tax among the property owners to attempt a dredging operation. In short, the problem was great and there was little hope for a solution.

Rutter asked for a chance to work on the problem. Our meeting took place in 1959 and from then until 1965, when the lake was completely rehabilitated, he overcame incredible handicaps. Just to name a few, over $115,000 had to be raised and not by a tax levy but by semi-voluntary contributions from the individual property owners. Only eighty percent participated in this. More than a million cubic yards of silt and water had to be removed from this lake through the complicated pontoon system, with a dredge digging into the lake and pumping the residue to shore over a mile-long pipeline. From time to time work completely stopped when the money supply dried up. At one point the weight of the water and the silt which was pumped to shore to clean the lake became so heavy that it disturbed the earth balance more than a quarter of a mile away from the spoil deposit area. As a result, utility poles were broken in half as their embedded bottom shifted while the tops were held in place by wires. Later, due to the displacement of the earth, a house split completely in half. Needless to say there were horrendous squabbles among the property owners' association.

The oil companies were solicited to allow the use of their gasoline to run the dredge at wholesale price, in return for advertising their products, and the same was true of several other products used in the enterprise. Since at no point in the clean-up project was there any financial security for the people working on it, it was a hand-to-mouth existence. The hard-working treasurer of the property association group, Jack Highland, who solicited funds day and night, ended up in the worst predicament. He had to pay withholding taxes on the employees' wages out of his own pocket, when funds were inadequate. Nevertheless, by 1965 the job was done. Fish multiplied in the lake, the boaters and water skiiers were happy and the sands on the beaches were pure white. It was a magnificent example of what community action inspired and enthusiastic leadership can do. The governmental contribution to the project was only the advice of various employees in the Highway and Conservation Departments of the state.

How often could this kind of community cooperative enterprise be successful? The absolutely essential ingredient was the resolute leadership and tireless energy of one man, Donald Rutter. Nevertheless, it proves the point that the people, individually and collectively, can do a great deal without governmental help, finance and supervision. True economy in government can only come from this kind of collective effort.

Very often a state official is told by his neighbor or another citizen that the way to reduce governmental costs and provide real economy is simply to curtail services. That is much easier said than done. I have given it a try on several occasions but without much success.

I attempted to restrict both the jurisdiction and number of persons required to man the License Appeal Boards. These boards are a very interesting legal entity. They provide a place for any errant driver to protest what he considers to be unfair treatment from the driver improvement service of the Secretary of State's office. For example, if a driver who has twenty-four points, including a couple of reckless driving convictions, thinks a sixty-day suspension is too rough a verdict, he has the right to go to the License Appeal Board. Unfortunately this legal mechanism is very expensive because it is required to be available for hearings in each county of the state, and the three-man board consists of a representative from the Secretary of State's office, one from either the Attorney General's office or the county Prosecutor's office, and one from either the local police or the sheriff's office. Needless to say, thousands of hours are required to hear these complaints. No other state in the country has any such appeal board available.

As it now stands in Michigan, the bad driver is given four chances. First, at the time he gets his violation ticket he can take it into the local traffic court, protest it and attempt to convince the judge that he is not guilty. Second, after he has amassed more than twelve points under the point system, he has an opportunity to appear before a Driver Improvement Officer of the State Department, and he can again protest individual tickets and hopefully avoid a suspension of his driving privilege. The third appeal is to the License Appeal Board, and the fourth, the circuit court. Here he can appeal for restoration of his license. In my opinion, four places to get off the hook for a bad traffic record is just one too many.

Thus, for several years I have tried, by amending the law, to do two things: first, to reduce the three-man trial board down to a one-man administrative operation which would save very substantial sums of money, and second to limit its jurisdiction to cases involving the implied consent law. Within the department we thought that this change would save seventy to eighty thousand dollars a year without considering the amounts of money it would save for the prosecuting attorney's office, sheriff or local police departments.

Unfortunately this attempt to cut down the License Appeal Board always died very quickly in the Legislature. I could never find any of the exponents of economy who would agree with me that its function should be sharply cut and its personnel reduced to save money.

XII

CAMPAIGN FUNDS

ONE of the responsibilities of the Secretary of State is to act as the Chief Elections Officer of the state. An enumeration of his duties is interesting. He prepares rules, regulations and instructions for the conduct of elections and registrations; he advises local elections officials, upon request, as to proper methods of elections; he publishes and furnishes a manual of instructions for the use of every election precinct; he publishes indexed pamphlet copies of election laws; prescribes and requires uniform forms; prepares the form of the ballot; requires reports from local election officials; investigates and reports violation laws; publishes the results of elections; and he supervises the bureau of elections within his own office assisted by a director, who is vested with the powers of the Secretary and performs the duties of the Secretary, under his supervision.

It was also his duty to receive and file reports of campaign expenses from candidates and committees, and to see to it that no candidate or committee spent more than the legal limit. In carrying out this duty, I became particularly interested in how campaign funds affected the success or failure of candidates and parties. In a close election, whether it be a primary or general election, if two candidates were about equal in ability and photogenic qualities, the winner would be the man who had a disproportionate amount of campaign funds at his disposal.

As a seven-time candidate for Secretary of State, I felt the need to set an example in regard to campaign funds. Therefore, I very consciously limited my spending during each of the seven elections. During my first candidacy in 1954, I spent slightly over $5,000, and in the last, in 1966, I spent a little over $18,000. In contrast, I was shocked at the candidate's expenditures in other state wide elections which sometimes amounted to several hundred thousand dollars. Nevertheless, Michigan is not alone in this respect. The larger states have candidates spending well into the millions. I believe the man who has the money or the means to raise the money has an advantage over other candidates in opposition to him. This is particularly true in regard to what political circles call "vanity votes." These are the extra votes, not needed to win, but make candidates look good in the eyes of his party or his constituents. For the last decade, newspaper polls can tell a candidate how he is doing from four to six weeks before an election, so that he can determine whether he wants to win or to win big.

If, for example, the polls show that he is winning by fifty-five percent a month before the election, he can relax his expenditures. However, if he wants to win by fifty-seven or fifty-eight percent (another hundred thousand votes) he probably will have to spend more than $100,000 on campaign expenditures. Since there is a limit of total campaign funds raised for all candidates, when one candidate gets a disproportionate amount of money from the public, it means that other lesser known candidates are going to suffer financially. In reality, candidates who have the money are able to sell themselves just as a manufacturer sells a new product.

I strongly felt there should be some way to limit the total amount of money being spent by candidates and/or political parties, and that an effort should be made to arrive at some kind of equality in the spending between the candidates. My mail indicated to me that the general public felt exactly the same way. Indeed, a 1968 Gallup Poll which asked the public whether they would favor or oppose a law putting a limit on the amount of money that could be spent *for* or *by* a candidate in his campaign, indicated that seventy-two percent of the Republicans favored a limitation, and sixty-five percent of the Democrats. My mail, I might say, indicated that one hundred percent of the people who wrote to me wanted some kind of limitation on spending.

The reader may say there already is a law on the books limiting the amount of expenditures. There is, indeed, a legal statute limiting campaign expenditures. Let me quote it for you.

(794) 168.902 Campaign expenses of candidates, limit, MSA 6.1902

Sec. 902. No sums of money shall be paid and no expenses authorized or incurred by or on behalf of any candidate to be paid by him in order to secure or aid in securing his nomination to any public office or his position in this state in excess of the amount computed at the rate of $40.00 for each 1,000 votes cast at the general November election in the last preceeding presidential year for the office of governor in the state or political subdivision thereof in which he is a candidate for nomination.

This law seems to say, if four million votes were cast in the previous general November election for the office of Governor, a candidate could now spend $160,000 in his campaign. Since the candidates were spending more than half a million dollars in their campaigns, obviously they were paying no attention to the intent of the law. The loophole is that phrase within the law which requires that the monies limited shall be "paid by him." No self-respecting candidate, under those circumstances, pays a large sum of money. He makes sure that the expenditures are paid by campaign committees in his behalf, who are not covered by the law. No Attorney General in my memory has ever prosecuted any candidate under this statute, and I doubt it will ever happen. Thus, we are going to have to look further for a means of limiting campaign expenditures.

Let us look at some of the expenditures both in Michigan and around the country.

First, a historical note. In 1846, Abraham Lincoln's friends raised a mere two hundred dollars to finance his race for Congress. After he won, Lincoln returned $199.25, having spent only seventy-five cents for a barrel of cider. In 1860, Lincoln won the presidency without making a single speech. His entire national campaign cost a hundred thousand dollars, a sum now barely sufficient for a thirty minute national telecast.

Now a presidential election will cost a candidate twenty million dollars or more, and while he is contesting for his party's nomination he may spend several million dollars more. A gubernatorial election in the populous states like New York, Pennsylvania or California will cost the candidate over five million dollars, excluding the cost of his primary campaign. The contest for U.S. Senator in the big states runs in the same financial league as the gubernatorial contest. Indeed, the expenditures in Michigan of a half million dollars for those two offices seem reasonable in comparison to some of the other states. However, in Michigan we have had expenditures as high as $50,000 for judicial races.

Now who are the people who make these contributions to build up campaign funds of millions of dollars? Most people think the Unions give large sums of money and the large corporate business interests do the same. I think that the total contributions of these two groups is rather small in the multi-million dollar national campaign fund contributions.

I take a rather cynical view of why people contribute. Certainly some contributors, those up to a hundred or a thousand dollars, may do so because they like the candidate or they like the party philosophy. But the large givers ($5,000 or over) want something in return for their contribution.

Senator Philip Hart phrased it in a more delicate manner in his Newsletter of August, 1966, when he said "Other contributions come from a source who 1, know from the candidate's statements that he will favor their interests; 2, know that the candidate does not favor their interests but hope that a contribution will relax his opposition; 3, want to make sure that they will at least have a chance to present their views if any adverse action is contemplated."

U.S. Senator Alan Cranston of California raises a nice question regarding the contributions that come from these large givers. "A moral question will arise in the minds of many candidates anytime a large contribution is proffered. If he accepts it how obligated will he be? One hard bitten answer often voiced among professional politicians in Sacramento our State Capitol runs like this 'If you can't take the lobbyists' money, eat their food, drink their booze and vote against them, you don't belong there.' "

Those who consider limiting, by law, the amount of money that any candidate, committee or political party can spend in a campaign must presuppose that some method can be used wherein an account of the receipts and disbursements of a campaign would be reported, so that the public will be aware of them. Here is the difficulty. There are a goodly number of people who contribute only if they are assured that their names will not appear on the public record. They do, however, want the *candidate* to know they are making the contribution. This is not only a Michigan problem, of course. Of the fifty states, only thirty-three of them have any methodology by law to force accounts of campaign expenditures and receipts and in no state does it work particularly well.

Often the candidate himself does not want it known that he is receiving contributions from a particular group or individual, so that in his accounting of expenditures and receipts which he files at the end of a campaign, he looks for a way to conceal those facts. Occasionally a donor of campaign funds will not want it known that he was contributing to a particular candidate simply because he was contributing to the opposition candidate as well. At other times he may feel his contribution will embarrass the candidate. Sometimes a political committee raising funds does not wish to file an account of their total expenditures because it will appear that they are far outspending their opposition. This would create a poor public image in the next political campaign.

Two very simple and legal loopholes are available to that kind of a donation. First, since the law requires that an accounting be made of political funds and contributions for "the campaign duration" the question of when the campaign took place is of great import. The accepted time of a campaign is from the filing date of the candidate to a period twenty days after the election, when the campaign financial reporting must be made. The solution becomes very simple. All that need be done is to raise the money the year before the candidate formally files his intention to run and, more importantly, to spend it at least a month before the candidate files. The easy way to do this is to hire an advertising agency and have them prepare campaign literature and television ads. In this way, all expenditures are made before the candidate files and need not be accounted for in the official filing document made after the election is over.

Another and maybe even simpler way to handle it is to give testimonial dinners for the candidate, and the large donors can buy one, two, or even five thousand dollars worth of tickets, at a hundred dollars a head, and assure those arranging the dinner that they will have few people there. Thus, a donor who gives two thousand dollars may only have two or three people at a hundred dollars each and the net profit for the candidate's committee will be very large. When an accounting is made after the election concerning amounts of money raised all it will show for this particular function will be "Testimonial Dinner for Candidate X, net receipts $27,000." In this way the donors' name will not appear on any campaign document.

Judging from these samples, it seems almost impossible to get a true accounting of the costs of any political campaign, and no state has been able to solve the total problem. The only place to my knowledge where a method has been developed to lessen campaign expenditures is in Great Britain, and I think it is worthwhile to take a look at their system.

Believe it or not, the last two Prime Ministers of Great Britain were elected with campaign funds limited to less than $3,000. All seventeen hundred candidates in the last British Parliamentary election had total funds limited to less than four million dollars. Of course, many things are very different. For one thing, and this is important, the British campaign is limited to seventeen days. Secondly, each candidate gets one free mailing to all his constituents, paid for by the Government. Third, he is limited to expenditures of two cents for each constituent within his district. Fourth, television is both free and equal. Each political party is allowed exactly the same amount of time at the same hour of the day.

I have over-simplified the picture of the British elections, but certainly it costs only a fraction of what an American election of like importance costs.

Having been personally involved in a great number of campaigns in my life, I have been subjected to a good deal of campaign oratory. One of the most fascinating speeches I have ever heard was by a candidate who had a very enthusiastic audience. The theme of his speech was equality. He was for "equality between black and white; between men and women; between queers and straights; between business and labor; between Anglo Saxons and Indians." But one place he was not in favor of equality was in campaign funds and campaign spending. At the end of his peroration, which was extremely well received, he said very frankly, "We have got to raise more money for my campaign than my opponent has because his name is a better known name than mine." The point he made is a good one. Campaign spending is not the only item in the political balance which determines elections. Obviously, the incumbent in office is usually a favorite. Also, the candidate sharing the nationality and religion of most of his constituents is favored. Certainly some names are a great political advantage, so that there seems to be no way to find true equality even after limiting campaign expenditures.

A fine example of the Machiavellian quality of campaign fund raising took place in 1969. It turned out to be a comedy of errors, but not to those involved. Since there are very few real secrets in the Michigan State Capitol between the two parties, I had heard rumors that the Republican high command was concerned about a Grand Jury taking place in Baltimore. I knew enough not to pay too much attention to the rumor mill, but this one seemed to persist and I listened carefully. The chief character in the play turned out to be Harold M. McClure, Jr., of Alma, who was the Republican National Committeeman from Michigan and also President of the McClure Oil

Company and prominent in the oil industry's fight to preserve its tax status. McClure was also President of the Independent Petroleum Association of America, so that he was wearing two hats most of the time; one as an oil man and one as a prominent and influential Republican.

Newspaper reports in September of that year reported that McClure had testified to the Grand Jury that he had made donations of about $90,000 to several prominent U.S. Senators of both parties. This, of course, caused an eruption in the Republican Party. Some prominent Republican legislators demanded that McClure resign. The leader in this effort was Senator Robert Huber. However, McClure's position was defended by the Republican State Chairman who argued that what a man did in the course of his private affairs was his own business, and not necessarily a part of his duties as Republican National Committeeman. The situation worsened when it was difficult to determine whether these were campaign contributions or gifts to friends of the oil industry. It became apparent that the entire $90,000 was not all McClure's money, but represented money given to him by people in the oil industry who wanted to help their cause with some of the Senators. Unfortunately for McClure, neither the people who gave him money for distribution in political circles nor the recipients of the money would admit to their part in the situation, although these were not illegal transactions. Possibly the Senators had either forgotten to report it as a political contribution, or to pay income tax on it if it was a gift.

Later, the newspapers reported that McClure was alleged to have given money to other Democrats including Senator Russell Long, Henry Jackson of Washington, Brewster of Maryland, as well as some Republicans. My interest was heightened, so that late in September I had Bernard Apol, Director of Elections, write to Harold McClure and ask if he were willing to make an accounting of the money he had raised and spent in the period from 1965 to 1968. I was not surprised at the prompt reply from Harold McClure saying that he felt "Due to considerable recent publicity and public conjecture over matters which I have heretofore believed to be of a personal nature, I would

rather not comment on any of these questions or make any suggestions at this time." Since I wished to pursue the matter, I wrote to
Governor Milliken and asked that he use his good office to have
Harold McClure make a financial accounting and report on the $90,-
000. The Governor's office replied very promptly and, as I anticipated,
declined to pressure McClure any further to make a disclosure. The
Governor did make a very pertinent statement in his letter. He said,
"I believe that the requirements of public disclosure should place the
onus of providing information on the financial recipient (office-holder)
rather than on the financial contributor (voter)." Since none of the
recipients were about to file any statements and since I had no legal
authority to subpoena such records, I gave up. After the incident, my
feeling was that Harold McClure was a stalwart battler for both the
Republican Party and the oil interests, and he was getting scant
support and little appreciation from his constituents.

There are many unsung and unhonored heroes in political campaigns. Among them the speech writers, the dinner givers, the fund
raisers, the schedulers and the secretaries in the campaign office. But
no one has a more responsible position in a campaign than the treasurer of the campaign funds. He has to account for the monies, pay
the bills and balance the books. I have been very fortunate for many
years to have the volunteer services of an old college schoolmate of
mine, Jack Linden, who heads the CPA firm of Linden, Klain, Israel
and Ross in suburban Detroit. Once he was in charge of things, I gave
no further thought to that part of any campaign, and my confidence
in him was certainly justified.

XIII

THE CAMPAIGN TRAIL

CAMPAIGNING in Michigan for statewide office is a most interesting experience. First, statewide elections are often very close between the political parties. Secondly, the size of the state is frightening when you have to cover all the counties. The procedure of the Democratic Party candidates for statewide office was to begin the campaign about the middle of September in an election year, and run it up to election day, the first week in November. This covered a period of approximately fifty days and since there are eighty-three counties, and several days have to be spent in the metropolitan area also, the statewide candidate has to get into two or more counties each day he is on the campaign trail. Because of the size of the state, the candidates are usually on the road for about five days at a time and then back to their home or to the capitol city for a day or two.

Few people know that Michigan geographically is one of the most difficult of all states to campaign in, and this is because of the long east-west axis of the upper peninsula, and the long north-south axis of the lower peninsula. When you are in Monroe County, you are closer to Washington, D.C. and New York than to towns in the west end of the upper peninsula, particularly if you travel by automobile. Needless to say, these circumstances cause substantial difficulties for the girls in the campaign office who have to set up schedules.

Since Governor Williams was a man of tremendous stamina, he set a very fast pace for the rest of us. He seemed to be able to go day and night for sixteen hours, and come up refreshed the following day. But even he wore down at times. I remember one instance when he had only twelve hours sleep in four days and tried to take a nap in a motel bedroom with twenty-five other people in the same room.

In 1958, our schedulers set up meetings in four towns in Macomb County for a most unholy trio, Philip Hart then running for the first time for the U.S. Senate; James O'Hara then running for the first time for Congress; and myself running for my third term. We were told to go to the main street of three different towns in Macomb County and go in and out of stores introducing ourselves and asking for support on election day. You can imagine the consternation of store owners when Hart, O'Hara and Hare walked in one after the other, introducing themselves and walking out immediately. The Mt. Clemens newspaper recorded our visits that year by saying the Democrats are trying to confuse the Republicans: Now that Hart, O'Hara and Hare have been in the county for a full twelve hours, no one in the county could identify any one of them separately.

One year my scheduler, Patti Knox, was sure I was in political trouble and she set up a backbreaking schedule for me. For a period of three days, I had fifteen to seventeen engagements in a day in five different counties. These were breakfasts, lunches, dinners, coffee klatches and plant-gate meetings. Also, if we had fifteen minutes to spare, we were to go to a shopping center and walk around and meet people. After two days of this schedule I thought I was physically breaking down, because it ended up each day with a plant-gate meeting when the midnight shift was beginning. This meant standing outside, usually in the rain and cold, as the men came off the afternoon shift. Most often they were so happy to get out of work that they simply ran past us without a second look. After one such experience, I was scheduled to appear at a plant gate in the next county, forty miles away, at 6 A.M. the following day. This entailed leaving one plant gate at 12:30 A.M. and driving forty miles to settle into a motel and sleep until 5:15 A.M. I protested strongly to the campaign office and was told, "We think you are in serious trouble and you do want to win." My rejoinder was, "not at the cost of my life." But it did no good. The schedule continued to be rigorous and day by day I became more tired. Finally, I solved my problem. Each night when I went to bed, usually around 1:00 A.M., I would call my scheduler at home and tell her I was through for the day. The next morning when I got up at 5:15 A.M. I would call again and tell her I was starting out. After only two days of these phone calls my schedule was revised and I was cut back to a sixteen hour day. It was a great improvement.

Quite often while on the campaign trail we would get a call from the office of the State Chairman, Neil Staebler, to report on the reaction to our visits of the previous day and perhaps offer some advice for our future travels. On one particular day there were five of us campaigning for state office and we ended up at a restaurant. The waitress came to our table and said, "A Mr. Staebler called and said 'don't touch the skin of the women.' " We were baffled by this cryptic observation and one of us called back to the State Chairman's office in Ann Arbor for enlightenment. There we found that the message had come from one of the aides in the office and the waitress was the only one in the restaurant at the time available to take the message. He reported to her that at least one of the candidates had been too profusive in his greetings to some of the women at a meeting, so he had tried to tell the waitress to relay the message that we should be reasonably restrained when meeting groups of women. Since the waitress, in conveying the message to us in a crowded restaurant, had said it in a very strong voice, I wondered whether we lost some votes in that community.

Because of Michigan's northern location, the scheduling for candidates had to be done so that most of the campaigning in the upper peninsula was done in the last two weeks in September. Then the candidates gradually moved down in conformity with the weather conditions to the top of the lower peninsula, the middle and finally for the last week or ten days, were confined to the lower tier of counties around the metropolitan area of Detroit. But weather was an all-important factor and often it seemed that in the upper peninsula rain and snow followed us even in late September. However, it is not surprising and most people do not realize that there are parts of Michigan that are north of Montreal and other parts west of St. Louis;

and that Marquette County is as large as the state of Rhode Island.

During a campaign all of us occasionally feared that if the election appeared to be close there might be some monstrous accusation made by our opposition in the last day or two of the campaign and time would not allow for an adequate refutation. This never happened but it demonstrated our fear about the fragility of a campaign and how relatively small and unimportant things can affect it.

One of the best demonstrations of how a small item can turn a campaign around took place in the 1950 gubernatorial campaign in which G. Mennen Williams ran against Harry Kelly, a three term Secretary of State, and a two term Governor. With approximately a month to go in the campaign, the public opinion polls showed that the candidates were about evenly matched with a fair number of undecided voters, but Kelly seemed to be gaining. Kelly had used a very pragmatic and persuasive campaign argument. Because Governor Williams was a member of the ADA (Americans for Democratic Action), which at that point was a strongly non-communist but liberal organization, Kelly intimated that Williams had what he called pinkish tinged viewpoints. He never made any direct accusations of Governor Williams' activities that would earn this particular adjective, but he was able to convey the suspicion and the newspapers picked up the image of Williams as a left winger. I felt bad about this very damaging accusation because I had been the first chairman of the Detroit ADA for three years, and I talked at one point to the Governor about resigning from the organization and getting out from under. He refused to consider that, and said that even if it cost a defeat he was not going to take that method of escape.

Paul Weber, the longtime and astute public relations and public information chief for Governor Williams, told the story:

> The National Republican Party had developed a campaign theme based upon 'Creeping Socialism.' It advised, indeed, virtually imposed, upon local candidates a campaign line seeking to show that the Democrats were socialists at heart and were generally, as you say, persons with 'pinkish tinged viewpoints.'
>
> Harry Kelly adopted this campaign theme. This, in my opin-

ion, was a very foolish thing for him to do because he had ready at hand a very effective campaign theme. He had been governor during World War II and we were in what looked like it might be the beginning of World War III, the Korean conflict. Williams was well liked but he had accomplished little in his first two years. Kelly could have, and should have, taken the line that Williams was a nice young guy but not adequate in the troubled times ahead when Michigan would need the tried and true hand of Harry Kelly at the helm. In the light of the eventual close outcome of the election, I think this might have elected Kelly. It would have been a very difficult line to counter.

Instead, Mr. Kelly harped throughout his campaign about Williams' membership in the 'socialist' ADA. We ignored this attack on the principle that by attempting to explain what the ADA was or to explain Williams' membership, we might only spread the poison. Toward the end of the campaign, however, it became clear that we could not ignore this charge. People were beginning to ask what the governor's explanation was for belonging to this subversive group. The implication that the ADA was a left-wing organization was beginning to sink in. It finally got to the point where the reporters covering the campaign were demanding that we respond to the ADA charge.

I felt that we had to respond and I issued a statement that we would 'dispose of' Mr. Kelly's ADA charges in a radio speech scheduled for about 10 days down the road. At that time, I had no idea *how* we would 'dispose of' this charge.

After some cogitation and staff consultation, it seemed to me that the best method was the method of 'innocence by association.' A study of the ADA's membership indicated that it had many fine persons associated with it (including one Jim Hare although this was not a name that we could use convincingly with doubtful or Republican voters in Michigan).

I wrote a speech draft based upon the 'innocence by association' psychology, listing many highly respected people—Mrs. Roosevelt, some nationally known clergyman, etc—and inquiring at the end of each paragraph: 'Does Mr. Kelly contend that this person is a Red?' The idea was to interpret Kelly's accusation of socialism as an accusation of communism. We felt that while many voters might be convinced that Williams was a socialist, very few could be convinced that he was a communist. When Kelly accused him of socialism, we would therefore show that he was not a communist. The speech sounded pretty good but it really lacked the kind of names with whom association would demonstrate innocence. With the exception of Eleanor Roosevelt, (and she was not universally beloved), we had no single person recognized by the general public as a person who could not be a Red.

I ended up, a few days before the promised 'disposal' of the issue, sitting in the campaign headquarters in the old Porter Hotel in Lansing wondering how I was going to make this rebuttal effective. Larry Farrell, the governor's executive secretary, was sitting nearby discussing some other aspect of the campaign with some campaign workers and I interrupted to ask him if he knew any other persons associated with the ADA who would be convincing to the Michigan electors as obvious non-communists. Larry said he didn't, but he added, 'Why don't you call Father Flanagan and ask him.' I said 'Why should I call Father Flanagan?' and Farrell replied, 'Why, he's a member.'

I went over to the telephone and called on Father Flanagan and put the question to him bluntly: 'Are you or are you not a member of the ADA?' He replied that he was. I told him that I was going to use that fact in the campaign speech. His attitude was that the truth should come out and that if he got any criticism from the Republican side that he would ask me to make clear that the initiative in the matter had come from us. He assured me that he would stand by his statement although he made the point that he did not participate in the purely political activities of the ADA. I then wrote the final page of the 'innocence by association speech,' disclosing that the pastor of the parish where Harry Kelly sent his children to school was a member of the ADA and ending with the question: 'Does Mr. Kelly contend that Father Flanagan was a Red?'

The speech did utterly 'dispose' of the only issue Mr. Kelly had. I was later told that Kelly was sitting in his hotel room in Detroit listening to Williams' speech and when he heard the final paragraphs about Father Flanagan, he jumped up from the chair and said to a close friend: 'What in the hell do we do now?' My informant tells me that the friend replied: 'Get ready for a continued experience in private life.'

In view of the outcome of the election it is clear that this speech caused sufficient damage to the Republican campaign to be decisive in the reelection of Williams. Father Flanagan did have some heat put on him from Republicans but the Bishop took the position he could see nothing wrong with Father Flanagan belonging to the ADA as long as he did not participate in their political endorsements. The Republicans consequently were never able to counter-attack successfully.

Father Flanagan was a stand up guy.

Kelly did not mention the pinko adjective for the rest of the campaign. I suspect that he thought he would win, from the way the public polls were going. Williams won an extremely close election in 1950, and he went through a five week recount before it was finally certified.

On the campaign trail the candidates very often hear disparaging remarks from the electorate about the doubletalk they allegedly use. On several occasions after a political meeting I have had a person in the audience question one of the speakers about what he as a candidate has had to say on a particular issue in another part of the state. The inference always was that he was saying one thing in southeastern Michigan and another thing in the upper peninsula. On occasion, of course, it did happen. Usually it was a matter of emphasis. But the candidate was in a peculiar position which the listener in the audience had no conception of. That is, he tended to have three choices on some issues. First, he had the position of his own conscience, whether he would go for proposition X or proposition Y. Secondly, he had the position of the constituents in his own district. This was particularly important if he was a legislator. Third, he had the position of the Democratic Party to take in consideration. On occasion those three positions were very far apart. I was interested in watching some of the candidates handle the question of open housing. One of them told me that personally he was in favor of open housing, but the constituency in his legislative district was completely opposed, and the position of the Democratic Party was in favor. He understandably altered his position depending on what kind of an audience he was talking to. The situation gave rise to a feeling of deep skepticism on the part of the voters.

During a political campaign in which the candidates are traveling with each other through several counties, they must be careful not to speak on the same subjects and the same issues. Therefore, the local candidates must select issues that are of consequence in that particular locality. The statewide candidates talked Michigan issues, the national candidates, such as the U.S. Senatorial candidate, talked about federal issues. As long as the candidates stick with generalities, cliches and image patterns, they have no troubles. The listeners love to hear the candidate say he will abolish poverty and bring about justice, reduce taxes and raise the standards of living while eliminating inflation and unemployment. But if the candidate discusses controversial issues, there is often a difference of opinion in the audience. Sometimes I have felt the audience only wanted to hear an evangelistic message, but did not want to talk about the basic methods of carrying out some of these wonderful proposals.

On two occasions, talking about one of my favorite subjects— economy in Government—I attempted to show the values of installing statewide computer networks with all the electronic devices that would not only save tremendous amounts of money, but would speed up the dissemination of information and abolish many very monotonous, routine jobs. Unfortunately, that is not what the people want to hear. I have had people openly yawn in my face when I made a pitch in that direction. I finally concluded that there was no political sex appeal in a computer, no matter how much money it saved or how much better it made the world in the end.

XIV

THE RECURRING QUESTIONS

THE Secretary of State's office, like the Governor's office, receives a great number of general questions about state government. Several of these questions recur year in and year out and come from all over the state and from members of both political parties. A great many come from students in political science classes at our universities. The one I probably received the most mail on was what I thought of the new Michigan Constitution.

The Constitution which took effect in 1963, after the Constitutional Convention had met the two previous years, replaced the seriously outdated 1908 version. Certain changes I certainly applauded.

1. The appointment of the State Auditor by the Legislature and not by election.

2. The establishment of a state Court of Appeals.

3. The elimination within five years of the Justice of Peace system.

4. The establishment of a Civil Rights Commission.

5. Consolidation of administrative agencies into not more than twenty departments.

6. A four year term for the Governor, Lieutenant Governor, Attorney General, Secretary of State, State Senators.

7. Tandem running of the Governor and Lieutenant Governor.

The greatest flaw in the new Constitution, I felt, was not something they did, but rather an omission. They made no change in the broad organized structure of state government. The new Constitution still retained separate Executive, Judicial and Legislative branches which allowed the checks and balances of government to deny any possibility of quick governmental action but, more importantly, it denied the voter and the public in general the ability to hold any single branch of government or any single person responsible for what was done or not done. The reason for the omission is certainly plain, although few of the delegates wanted to discuss it. The forces of precedence, the traditions of history and the difficulty of selling a new concept of governmental organization were so great, I am sure, that no delegate wanted to get into that kind of a fight. However, I still feel until we can centralize both authority and responsibility in our state government we are going to, as the British say, "muddle through."

A second recurring question came almost entirely from Michigan's Democrats. This was, "why it is since we now have a one man one vote apportionment of our legislative districts that the Democrats, when they have a total majority vote in the state, do not have a majority of the seats in the legislature?" This question, of course, demonstrates that most people do not understand what apportionment or reapportionment of legislative seats means. Under the Gus Scholle one man one vote proposal, which finally became law, it only meant that each legislative district, whether it be in the Senate or the House, would have approximately the same population. But this alone would not guarantee the Democrats a majority of the seats in the Legislature, even if the total vote for all offices state wide was better than fifty percent in the Democratic favor. The reason for this is that the Democrats have pockets or districts in which they win big, by eighty-five or ninety percent, so that the Republicans might have only forty-eight percent of the total vote, but they win more close seats than the Democrats, and thereby have a majority of members in both Houses of the Legislature. Indeed, by any computation, the Democrats need at least fifty-four percent of the total state vote in order to break even on legislative seats.

A third very persistent question in the last years has been, "what happened in the Detroit primary and November election that caused the late reporting of the election results," and a secondary question, "is the computerized system a good one?"

I must give a very cautious answer to this loaded question. First, the system can be made to work with very intensive training of the personnel and adequate supervision. It works in other places in the country and in Midland, Michigan. It entails bringing voting cards which have been punched by the voters from the polling places to a centralized computer for counting and, because of that, it is not necessarily a quicker method of obtaining voting results. By the old method of using voting machines, the results of the tally were often called in by phone from the polling place to a central office and would be tabulated there. The costs of the computerized electronic voting mechanisms are substantially less than for the highly complicated voting machines previously used and this, of course, is a plus for the new method.

However, I have one substantial fear and reservation about the new method. That is, its operation is extremely centralized in the final counting at the central computer. This means that the programmer who sets up the computer to do the vote counting can, by means of his programming operation, set it to favor a particular candidate or proposition and, worse than that, it is almost impossible to detect such an effort on his part. Therefore, the probity of this whole system comes down to a single man at a computer center without the usual vote-challengers operating at a polling place to keep the count honest. Assuming that there will never be a problem of honesty on the part of any programmer, I see no reason why the system cannot work.

An interesting footnote to this question is a recital of how computerized voting came about in Detroit. In 1969, Al Fishman, Chairman of the New Democratic Coalition (NDC), joined a small two-year-old consulting firm known as Management Engineering Corporation, which specialized in information and control systems.

Fishman and his NDC colleagues worked hard in the fall of 1969 for the election of George C. Edwards III, as Clerk of the City of Detroit. After Edwards took office on January 1, 1970, Fishman approached him and suggested Detroit needed an electronic computer operated voting mechanism for use in its elections. He recommended the punch-card voting equipment sold by a Texas corporation. The deal was concluded in late spring, the city purchased $843,000 worth of equipment and Fishman was the salesman of record.

The punch-card system worked poorly for Detroit in both the August primary and the November general election. Detroit officials angrily debated whether to return the equipment and scrap the entire system. Edwards' political future, at least for the moment, was put in serious jeopardy. Meanwhile, Fishman sued to collect the twenty-five thousand dollars sales commission he said the company owed him for his services.

The fourth general question which came in in great volume was, "where do we get information on laws relating to driving?" The average driver has no idea of the number of laws restricting, constricting, and limiting him. The Point system is not understandable to many drivers; the Financial Responsibility Law is a morass; the method of collecting from the MVACF is a mystery; the Implied Consent Law is an enigma to many drinking drivers. What reports need a driver make after an accident? Because a majority of these requests for information came from the Detroit area, my good deputy Walter Elliott recommended that we set up a drivers' clinic to counsel with drivers who were revoked or suspended from their driving privilege. This we did, and it turned out to be a great success because many of the Detroit traffic court judges recommended that persons appearing before them make a trip to the clinic and learn what the laws are all about. We quickly found out that there were a fair number of drivers who were off the road simply because they did not comply with some technicality of the law. A fifteen-minute counselling session served to straighten them out and certainly prevented them from getting in any deeper. In total, the Seven Mile Road Clinic of the Secretary of State's Motor Vehicle Division has been an outstanding success.

XV

TRAFFIC SAFETY

BEFORE taking office in 1955, I was neither concerned nor greatly impressed with the problem of traffic safety. I felt that deaths, injuries, and accidents inevitably took place in Michigan. If four or five million people drive cars in the state, it was one of the penalties of having that many people on the roads. My viewpoint on the subject was drastically changed by one man—Governor Williams. In the two months between my election in November of 1954, and taking office January 1, 1955, the Governor talked to me on three occasions long and seriously about the enormity of the problem. His interest and concern were certainly contagious because from that day on I became very concerned about the problems of traffic safety.

The statistics of the problem are impressive enough. Each year we can expect twenty-three or twenty-four hundred people to die in accidents; and more than three hundred thousand reported accidents. Many go unreported because the participants in the accidents do not want their insurance companies to hear of the mishap. A very interesting contrast is that the deaths of Michigan persons in the Vietnam war do not equal one-tenth of the deaths on the highways, whether it be a month or a year or a succession of years. The cost of this carnage on the highway will run better than one million dollars a day.

Before even suggesting solutions to the problem, let us look at some facts. How does Michigan compare with other states, particularly the industrial states like California, Pennsylvania and New York? In comparison, Michigan is neither good nor bad. Half the states in the country have a better record and the other half have a worse record. The method of determining between states as to what is a good or bad record, I think is worthwhile reporting on. The comparison is made by determining in each state the number of deaths per hundred million miles driven in that state. The mileage driven is determined by the amount of gas used by autos in the state. Thus a record of six deaths or more per hundred million miles driven in a state is very bad and, on the other hand, a record such as Connecticut might have of three or four deaths per hundred million miles is very good. Michigan has tended to be in the neighborhood of four to five deaths per hundred million miles driven.

Statistically we know a good deal about fatalities. We know where the accidents happen, when they happen, the conditions under which they happen and the kind of persons involved. For example, we know fatalities will be down in January, February and March each year because driving conditions are so bad that high speeds are not as common as they are in the summer months. Indeed, the month of June is probably the worst of the whole year because people drive much faster. We know that the worst hour for fatalities is between 1 and 2 A.M. This is the time when people are going home from parties or when the bars are closing, and it points out the particular problem of the drinking driver. We know that roads have a great effect on the fatality toll. The freeways have an excellent record in contrast to country roads.

We also know a good deal about the particular kind of driver who is most often involved in a fatal traffic accident. He is a person that I would term an "incorrigible bad driver." Let me cite at some length the record of one particularly incorrigible driver that we dealt with over a period of years. This man, whom I shall call JNH, was a thirty-six year old man who, in the period of nine years in Michigan, amassed one of the worst records to be found in our files. He was murdered at the age of thirty-six in 1967, while trying to collect a gambling debt.

Over a period of years, he was convicted of forty-seven moving traffic law violations, on five occasions he was convicted of reckless driving, and he was convicted five times of speeding twenty miles or more over the speed limit. In the two years before his death, he had accumulated forty-five points as the result of nineteen traffic law violations. Between 1958 and 1967 he had a cumulative total of one hundred and thirty-seven points against him. His license was first revoked in 1964. Yet he never, except for the time he served in jail, ceased driving for a single day so far as we could discover. Between 1955 and 1967 he served at least two hundred and fifty-three days in Michigan jails and paid at least seven hundred and sixty-five dollars in fines. In addition to his Michigan traffic record he also had eight convictions for traffic illegalities in Atlanta, Georgia. He also had a criminal record for such crimes as assault and battery, illegal operation, breaking and entering mail boxes, unlawfully driving an auto and investigation for robbery. Since he was also involved in several accidents and had judgments rendered against him for damages done to other parties which he did not pay, he was denied the privilege of titling and owning a car. He continued to drive during this entire nine year period in cars owned or titled in other people's names. Although at one point he did register cars in one of his six assumed names.

The record illustrates this man's disregard for motor vehicle—and other—laws. A court reporter relates that "he states he has never worked regularly for anybody but himself. He states he is a professional gambler and hustler and lives by his wits."

Needless to say the state and our own department failed in attempting to effect any kind of conformity upon this man. His traffic antics cost the state many thousands of dollars in court trials, legal prosecutions and jail terms. It is evident that the State Department was unable to handle this man, to control, reeducate or to change him. The fact is that his record was getting worse year by year and at the time of his death it was almost inevitable that he would have been involved in fatalities on the highway had he lived. While JNH was an exceptionally bad driver, there are thousands like him with records perhaps not quite as bad yet but who potentially could produce even worse ones. The fact is that one out of seventy Michigan drivers fits into the category of "incorrigible driver."

One of the characteristics of the "incorrigible driver" is that he seems to be in trouble across the entire social spectrum. Not only do sixty percent of these drivers have police records and they all read about the same—failure to pay alimony, drunk and disorderly, disturbing the peace, etc. When called in to discuss their records, they all confess to the same kind of habits—inability to get along with others, trouble with their spouses, neighbors, bosses and even with their children. It becomes apparent that little can be done to rehabilitate them strictly from a traffic safety standpoint. They are simply abnormal personalities and their defects simply show up more clearly in their driving record than any place else.

Sometimes consideration of a particular driver's record had a rather wry humor about it. For example, a man who was involved in a fatality when his passenger died after his car hit a barricade, was asked to explain what happened. It was pointed out to him that before he hit the barricade, he had passed three very large signs saying "Barricade Ahead." His answer was short and simple. He said "I thought they said barbecue ahead and I was in a hurry." He simply underlined one of our great problems: about two percent of the drivers in our state are illiterate and unable to read anything but the simplest signs. Their driving records show this since they get many traffic tickets for offenses such as making improper left turns, simply because they cannot read the sign and have no idea that they are breaking the law. In Detroit the State Department attempted to overcome this difficulty by establishing, in cooperation with the Detroit School System, a reading course which concentrated only on a limited number of traffic signs and signals. This produced some very gratifying results.

A special kind of "incorrigible driver" needs special consideration —the alcoholic. In 1956 it was believed that alcoholics caused about one-fourth to one-third of all fatalities in the country. But many experts in the traffic field thought they were a far greater menace than those figures indicated. I ordered a special investigation of a random one thousand fatalities to be investigated and to determine what the driver involved, and perhaps at fault, had been doing before the fatality occurred. That investigation brought out some very interesting facts. First of all, it could be proven that more than six hundred of the thousand had been drinking before the fatality took place. Only about two hundred of those drivers could be proven not to have been drinking previous to the time of the fatality. The other two hundred cases were impossible to determine, usually because the driver had been away from either home or business for some hours previous to the fatality and no one was available to say whether they had been drinking or not. However, that investigation convinced me that the alcoholic driver was a far greater menace than had been indicated. Two-thirds of the fatalities investigated in the survey showed that they occurred on rural roads at early morning hours when traffic was very light.

The law then, as now, made it mandatory that anyone convicted of drunk driving would have his driving privilege and license revoked, which in practice meant that they could not reapply for reinstatement as a driver for at least ninety days. The question became what to do about the alcoholic driver. He cannot control himself or his drinking habits. Investigation further showed that alcoholics were a cross section of the total population. Less than three percent of them would be called derelicts, and many of them held very responsible jobs, although their drinking habits had tended to hold them back from promotion or success in those jobs. I determined that the best thing I could do was to attempt, through our department, to talk to these people about their alcoholic problems and to have them, through their own efforts, attempt to rehabilitate themselves. This was much easier said than done, since many or most alcoholics would deny that they were alcoholics. Dr. Richard Bates of Lansing developed certain criterion to determine who is an alcoholic. If the individual involved fitted this criterion, it was explained to him and hopefully he would recognize his problems and do something about them.

The following is taken from the Michigan Driver Improvement Program Guide for Identifying the Alcoholic at the Interview:

> Observe a red-faced untidy appearance, lack of self-confidence, and some puffiness around the eyes. Be on the look out for any tremor of the hands, fingers that are stained with ciga-

rette smoke and any slight scars from burns between the first and second fingers which hold cigarettes. Note whether the person is tatooed. Almost without exception every tatooed female is an alcoholic. More than half of all alcoholics are highschool drop-outs. More than half of all alcoholics are not living with their first spouse but have remarried, often to another alcoholic. Be suspicious of anyone living at a downtown address which usually indicated the person lives close to the core center of the city, usually in substandard housing. Alcoholics tend to be immoderate in everything. Inquire into their habits of smoking, coffee intake, work, diet and sleep. Nine out of ten alcoholics are heavy cigarette smokers. Ask the subject if he sometimes drinks too much, or more than his wife thinks he ought to. Ask if he drinks in the morning. If in his defense an alibi is encountered, you are likely looking at an alcoholic. A person who admits to 8 beers or 8 ounces of whiskey at a sitting probably is an alcoholic and an almost 'never fail' test question is to ask whether the subject has had blackouts while drinking after age 22. If he admits he did, he is almost certainly an alcoholic. Do not confuse the word 'blackout' with intoxication. Ask the subject, do you sometimes get drunk without meaning to. After age 25 male social drinkers seldom get drunk without meaning to, and female drinkers almost never.

In checking on the medical history of the driver find out what his caloric intake is and if you find that only a few hundred calories a day come from food, you can be suspicious he is getting calories from alcohol. Tuberculoses can be an important clue. Alcoholics have 5 times as much tuberculosis as the general population. Nearly half the persons in TB hospitals are also alcoholics. There seems to be a definite association between the two diseases. Alcoholism is most prevalent in Roman Catholics of Irish extraction. The second largest nationality group is persons of Polish extraction. The least likely is Jewish. Alcoholism is almost never found in persons of the Jewish faith.

Ancestry is also important. About 50% of all alcoholics have one alcoholic parent. The work record of an alcoholic is generally poor, with many of them going from one job to another. The occupations with high incidence of alcoholism are house painters, salesmen and bar tenders. About 50% of all alcoholics have arrest records for one or more charges of being drunk and disorderly.

Another Michigan medical man who has added a great deal to our knowledge of the drinking driver is Dr. Melvin Selzer of the University Hospital in Ann Arbor. Dr. Selzer developed MAST (Michigan Alcoholic Screening Test) which has been able to do a great deal in differentiating between the social drinker and the alcoholic. He has also demonstrated that our great problem in traffic safety is not with the social drinker but with the true alcoholic, and nothing short of reformation of this individual will help alleviate a desperate situation. One of the better signs of the times is that alcoholic rehabilitation schools are developing throughout the country and I believe that nine of these schools will soon be operational in Michigan, subsidized by matching federal funds from the U.S. Department of Health.

Some alcoholic drivers attempt to get psychiatric help, a few of them stop drinking altogether, but the great majority of them simply ignore the advice and help or deny they are alcoholics. Unfortunately, one thing that most of them have in common is a determination to continue driving whether their license is suspended, revoked or cancelled. I looked through many records of alcoholics who had been convicted of drunk driving from six to fifteen times, and were revoked far into the future; yet they continued to drive in spite of the fines and jail sentences. The answer to the alcoholic problem has not yet been reached.

During the early years of my administration, the law enforcement authorities had a good deal of trouble in trying to arrest and bring about the conviction of a drunk driver. For years the only way a patrolman could identify a drunk driver was by some kind of objective personal evaluation such as observing erratic driving patterns, slurred speech or a flushed face, or requiring the driver to walk a straight line. But such tests, it was well-known by policing agencies, are highly unreliable. It sometimes brought about the conviction of a perfectly innocent driver who either was under medication or who had a nervous disability that gave him the appearance of being drunk. Also, it left policemen open to the charge of having a personal grievance against the driver, racial discrimination or local political pressures, rather than a true driving arrest. Fortunately, in 1968 the Implied

Consent Law came into affect in Michigan. It means in effect that when a person takes out an operator's license he consents to take a chemical test: blood, urine or breathing, if arrested for drunk driving. If he refuses, which is his right, his license can be suspended. The law also stipulates a "presumptive blood level of intoxication." In the case of Michigan, this is .15, which is fifteen-hundredths of one percent of alcohol in the blood. This law has worked rather well in Michigan, in my opinion. It has taken the guess-work away from the law enforcement officer so that when the suspected drunk driver is brought in for a chemical test, and in Michigan that means a breathalyzer test, the machine makes the decision as to whether or not he is drunk.

The drinking driver, of course, is not just Michigan's problem, it is a national and international one. Michigan's "presumptive blood level of intoxication" is very lenient as compared with twenty-five other states who comply with the recommended national standard of .10. I would suspect that in the next year or two, Michigan will adjust to this national standard.

I cannot leave the discussion of the Implied Consent Law without commenting on how well the State Police handle the very difficult situation of bringing in the drunk driver and administering the breath-alyzer test. Having discussed the errant driver at some length, the question is what to do about him. The citizenry has many suggestions and resolutions and I have personally received literally hundreds of letters containing advice. It has been suggested that every bad driver have a special tag on his car; that all drivers under twenty-one be prohibited from driving; that all drivers over sixty-two be prohibited; that women be eliminated from the road; that drunk drivers be given the death sentence; that all cars more than five years old be prohibited from the roads, and finally that no one be allowed to drive unless they are a college graduate. Incidentally, I must defend the record of the aged driver. The facts are that drivers sixty-five and over have a good driving record and I wish I could say as much for the people from eighteen to twenty.

The Federal Government, too, has some recommendations on traffic safety. Indeed, their recommendations are quasi-mandatory. The Federal National Highway Safety Bureau, which is a part of the U.S. Department of Transportation, has made sixteen separate recommendations on safety and have admonished the states that if they do not follow these standards, the Federal Government will withhold some of the monies now given to the states for highway construction. The state of Michigan conforms with a majority of these sixteen standards and like many other states we would like to conform with more. However, some of them are very expensive to put into effect. Here are some of the more important recommendations.

The first is that Michigan should have yearly motor vehicle inspection for every vehicle in the state. The intent of this is to get the old automobiles off the road or to get them fixed so that they are reasonably safe to drive. Michigan is less than perfect in conformity with this recommendation, since we have what is called random inspection administered by the State Police. Under this procedure the State Police set up roadside testing devices and pull over likely looking suspects and test them on the spot. Unfortunately, its effectiveness covers less than ten percent of all the cars in the state in any year.

Recommendation two suggests that motor vehicle registration be improved and adequate records developed so that vehicle ownership can be identified rapidly and efficiently for investigative and law enforcement purposes. In this respect the computers in the State Department are doing a fine job and we are in conformity with the federal recommendation.

Recommendation four is that each state shall set up a driver education program in the high schools. Michigan probably has one of the very best driver education programs anywhere in the country. Unfortunately, the effect of that program seems to wear off rapidly and the accident and violation rate of the eighteen to twenty year old drivers is extremely high. Somewhere we have failed. Indeed, Professor David Klein of Michigan State University says that driver education as now taught in Michigan does not significantly reduce the number of accidents. He argues that the sons of bad drivers tend to be bad drivers, and that somehow driver education in the high schools has not been able to give the students the mature attitude necessary to be a reasonable driver.

Recommendation five sets standards for drivers license examining and Michigan is in substantial conformity here.

Recommendation ten concerns record-keeping, both on accidents and on drivers. Michigan is very well in conformity with this standard and particularly since the full use of computers came into effect. The record of any driver can be transmitted all over the state in a matter of seconds. This, of course, is extremely important to the law enforcement officer who is holding a motorist on the road, and radios in to his post to ask for the person's background and driving record.

Recommendation eleven is one in which Michigan and other states in the country are very remiss. That is in getting emergency medical services to the injured party at the scene of an accident. In some places in Michigan an accident victim can be picked up and taken to a hospital in a matter of minutes after the accident. However, in other places, particularly in the rural areas, it may be a period of hours before the victim can be hospitalized.

Recommendations twelve and thirteen have to do with highway design, construction, maintenance and adequate traffic devices. Michigan, again, at least in contrast to many other states, is in very good conformity with the standards.

I perhaps have a vested interest in seeing to it that Michigan should adopt the federally recommended standards since for several years I was a member of the National Highway Safety Advisory Commission. This group met several times a year in Washington D.C., made recommendations and passed judgments when these various standards were being considered. I was certainly highly impressed with the caliber of the twenty-nine member Commission appointed by the President.

Although the average citizen thinks that deaths, accidents and injuries are almost inevitable, he does not realize the tremendous cost to him personally if he is a driver. It appears that the total cost of accidents, insurance, etc., in Michigan during 1971 will cost more than five hundred million dollars. Divide that sum by the five million drivers in Michigan and you will see on an average how much each driver must pay. He does not pay that sum directly to the repairman or the insurance company, necessarily, but he pays it indirectly in welfare taxes for families who have lost the breadwinner, to hospitals who must have charity wards for the injured, to municipalities for property damage done in accidents, to penal institutions for the incarceration of drivers and to alcoholism clinics that attempt to do something about the alcoholic driver.

One of the benefits that comes out of the computer complex which the Secretary of State's office has is that it contains, for ready reference, the records of all the five and one-half million drivers in Michigan. Those records are available to anyone who is willing to pay two dollars per record for a copy. This year I suspect that close to three hundred thousand inquiries will be made into that system, the majority of them, of course, by insurance companies wanting to check on the record of the insured, but an increasing number of inquiries are coming from employers who, before hiring or promoting a candidate for a job, want to know more about him. Incidentally, a driving record is the cheapest, quickest, easiest kind of a criterion by which to make a judgment about a person. I wonder just how many persons have been turned down in their quest for liability insurance, in their desire for a job or a promotion simply because a driving record was available to either their insurance company or their employer.

To get back to the central theme, what to do about the great problem of traffic safety, I have two very unorthodox suggestions to make. Neither one of the two have much hope of accomplishment, but I think they are worthwhile discussing. The first suggestion is to put all authorities and jurisdictions that have anything to do with traffic safety in one basket and under one head. This would include the record-keeping section of the Secretary of State's office, the traffic court judges, the police authorities who have the road patrols, and the penal institutions that hold the convicted driver. This may provide uniformity of enforcement in the traffic safety area. As it now stands, the police department may have too much of a crime problem to put many men on the road patrol. Or judges, recognizing that the penal facilities are too limited, will not jail an errant driver. Needless to say none of these jurisdictions would want to surrender the authority they now have and go under a central head, so I see little hope of accomplishment with this kind of an unorthodox suggestion.

My second suggestion deals with the incorrigible driver. We have noted that nothing that has been done by state or local authorities has had much effect on this person. Whether he is suspended or revoked he continues to drive. He will pay tremendous amounts of money in fines and even serve five and ten day sentences but the minute he is out of jail he is back behind the wheel of a car. Under these circumstances my suggestion is that any driver who is convicted of driving while his license is either suspended or revoked shall have the vehicle he is driving confiscated by the state. We have a law on the books, which is very seldom used, that states that the car may be impounded if the driver's license has been revoked. However, the car must belong to the driver involved, which means that since many of them drive cars titled in other persons' names, it has little effect. I recognize this would be a most controversial law because in too many instances the car would belong to a person other than the driver and the owner would pay the penalty. However, it would certainly make people more careful as to whom they lend or rent cars and in the long run I suspect it is the only way of controlling the incorrigible driver.

During my sixteen years in office it was incumbent upon me to revoke or suspend hundreds of thousands of drivers licenses. In the mid-1950's this was being done at the rate of about a hundred thousand a year, by 1970 it was well over two hundred thousand. Since the notice of revocation in letter form went out from our office it tied me very closely to that revocation, and some of my political colleagues warned me that the million or more persons who had their licenses revoked would wake up some election day and remember my name with distinct aversion. However, the predictions of my colleagues never manifested themselves. After my first two elections, which were close, the next five I won by very comfortable margins, and never saw any signs that the unhappy drivers were voting against me. In 1970 a survey was taken to determine the personal characteristics of incorrigible drivers and one of the facts that came out was that very few of this particular group vote in any election and, more than that, a relatively small percentage of them were even registered to vote.

XVI

M.V.A.C.F.

THESE initials stand for Motor Vehicle Accident Claims Fund which was set up in 1965 to reimburse the innocent victims of accidents who could not receive compensation for their injuries in any other way. However, its birth and development previous to that time is an interesting story.

Late in 1956, a woman came to my office with a plea for help. Her story was a sad one. Three years before, her husband had been standing on the curb on Woodward Avenue in Detroit when a motorist swerved up over the curb, struck him, drove on and was never identified. Her husband suffered a spinal injury which left him paralyzed from the shoulders down and at the time of her visit he was bedridden in the Wayne County General Hospital and presumably would remain there for the rest of his life. The economic consequences to that family were catastrophic. They had four children; the oldest one had been forced to drop out of college; the mortgage on their home had foreclosed; their total savings were used for medical costs in the first six months after the accident. They were thereafter destitute and were on the welfare rolls. This woman's plea to me was to ask why there was not a governmental means of securing compensation to innocent victims of an accident like her husband's.

After some thought on the matter, I resolved that I would attempt to set up a fund somehow, somewhere, within the state governmental unit to provide a means of reimbursing innocent victims. Little did I know the path I had chosen. I announced my intent to do something about the problem at a luncheon group in Detroit which was covered by the press. They gave it fairly wide coverage and the response was almost immediate. First of all, I had a succession of letters and phone calls from families who had suffered from the same type of accident situation as the woman had told me about. But, secondly, I immediately found that the automotive insurance companies were totally opposed to any such plan. It was months before they solidified their objections and reported them to me in concrete form. Meanwhile, I had a steady flow of letters coming in which highly approved of the plan, most of them having been victims of this same situation. There was some favorable editorial comment in newspapers but, on the other hand, nobody in government came forward to espouse the ideal and the idea, and certainly no one in the Legislature made motions of trying to put this plan in legislative bill form.

I knew a fair amount about the pitfalls of reimbursing innocent victims or, indeed, the total problem of automobile liability insurance since I was the administrator of the Financial Responsibility Act, a law which had been on the Michigan books for many years. The intent of this law was to encourage, or indeed to force, all motorists to buy liability insurance so that in the event they were negligent in an accident and caused injuries, the innocent victim could be reimbursed through their insurance policy. The method used by the law to force the motorist to secure liability insurance was primarily by punishing him after the accident. If he was unable or refused to pay the damages to the other party, then his drivers license was revoked until he complied with any financial judgment made against him in the courts. The method which the law used to insure compliance was to require that all motorists involved in accidents of over two hundred dollars must file an accident report with the Secretary of State's office. In that report they had to show their financial responsibility primarily by proving that they had liability insurance to protect the other motorist. In the event they did not carry liability insurance they were notified by the Secretary of State's office that they must get such insurance or their drivers license would be revoked. This had a very salutory effect on many uninsured motorists and they would buy liability insurance.

But the weakness of the law still lay in the fact that this, in no way, would guarantee that the innocent victim of an accident would get compensation. In fact, the name given to the Financial Responsibility Act by one person was the "One Free Accident Law." Another weakness of the Financial Responsibility Law was that it could do nothing for the victim of a hit-and-run accident since there was no one to punish, no one to sue, and for many pedestrians no possible way of receiving financial restitution for their injuries.

Early in 1957 I began an investigation of what the other states and the Canadian Provinces were doing about this problem. I found their problems were almost exactly the same as ours and I particularly investigated the laws in New York, Maryland, New Jersey, Ontario and Saskatchewan, because they seemed to have made well-formulated attempts to deal with the difficulty. At the same time, I was receiving many letters from my constituents who advocated compulsory insurance as the answer. They argued that if everyone was forced to carry liability insurance, there would be no problem. Therefore, I added the state of Massachusetts to my list of places to be investigated since they had had a compulsory auto insurance law for more than forty years. I found the executive in charge of the compulsory insurance program in Massachusetts was most dissatisfied with the way the program was operating. First of all, he said there was no means of forcing people to buy and keep compulsory insurance. Some drivers were insured on one day for sure—the day they bought their license plates. The day after, they would lapse on their premium payments and, therefore, became automatically uninsured. Secondly, having compulsory insurance did nothing for the victims of hit-and-run accidents.

Next, I looked into the Maryland laws and found that in their efforts to make the uninsured motorist buy insurance, they demanded that, if he had no liability insurance at the time he bought license plates, he had to pay a fee of seventy dollars per year. As a result, forgery of insurance policies and insurance certificates became widespread.

The province of Saskatchewan had a very unique situation. The government itself carried the liability insurance, rather than private insurance companies, and the cost was incorporated in the registration charge for a vehicle at the time the motorist bought his plates. I knew without investigating further that a governmental insurance company would find vast opposition in the Legislature in this state, and dropped my investigation of Saskatchewan. However, I found three places where one plan was working out well. These were New Jersey, New York and Ontario. In all three the primary cost of building up the fund to reimburse innocent victims was paid by the uninsured motorist at the time he bought his license plates. All three of the commissioners in these states had the same complaint—many motorists are insured when they buy their plates but are not insured for the rest of the license plate year, either because they cancel their own insurance or have trouble with their insurance company and are cancelled out.

Late in 1957, I publicly announced that I had completed my investigation and that in 1958 I would introduce a bill into the Legislature using the best aspects of the plans I found in New York, New Jersey and Ontario. At this point the wrath of the auto insurance companies descended upon me. They strongly objected to any of my proposals and had three major arguments. First, the already existing Financial Responsibility Law took care of all but a small number of victims. This, of course, I did not believe. Second, they argued that it would be putting the state of Michigan in the insurance business, which would be in conflict with private industry, and we might move along to the situation of Saskatchewan where the state itself was the insurance company. Third, they used what I called a statistical argument. The auto insurance companies argued that there were relatively few uninsured drivers, that by their figures it was only three or four percent of the driving population, which at that time would have meant a hundred and twenty to a hundred and sixty thousand uninsured drivers. I argued that the number of uninsured drivers was closer to ten percent of the driving population, and I based my figures on the fact that more than ten percent of the motorists who made reports of accidents showed that they were uninsured at the time of the accident. Admittedly, it could be argued that bad drivers would be the uninsured drivers and drivers involved in accidents would necessarily be more uninsured than non-accident prone drivers. Neither one of us could prove our points because automobile insurance companies do not know the exact number of people whom they insure. They only tabulate the money they receive in premiums and the money they pay out, which is what the insurance commissioner of the state demands. I felt this debate was a stand-off and, therefore, meaningless.

A law setting up funds to reimburse innocent victims of accidents should have certain broad objectives. First, to reimburse that victim as quickly as possible; second, to encourage motorists to carry liability insurance; third, the fund should take care of catastrophic costs in accidents rather than fender scraping accidents—for that reason I wanted a minimum limitation of at least two hundred dollars in damages before a claim could be filed. My reason for that was that a fifty dollar claim filed with this fund would require more than fifty dollars worth of investigation and the total proceeds within the fund would be spent in administrative costs. Fourth, I felt the new law should require the negligent or guilty party to reimburse the fund perhaps over a period of time, but make sure that the victim received his compensation quickly. Fifth, the fund should be financially self-sustaining and motorists who were protected by it should pay the cost rather than try to exist on legislative appropriations. Sixth, to facilitate collections, any fees should be paid by the motorist at the time he purchases his license plates. Seventh and last, I hoped we could safeguard the fund against fradulent claims.

When I publicly announced my objectives and my intention to enter a bill in the 1958 Legislature setting up this fund, I received a deluge of mail almost completely favorable to the idea. But again I was remarkably impressed by the lack of activity among governmental units. No legislator spoke up to volunteer help in the passage of the bill, no governmental executive from the Governor on down announced he would support the bill, but there were a fair amount of editorial comments in the newspapers which were favorable to the intent of this kind of bill.

One attorney did volunteer his services, and to him I shall always be grateful for his legal advice. He was Harold Norris, now professor of law at the University of Detroit Law School. Between 1958 and 1965, he spent innumerable hours drafting and redrafting a bill to establish a fund in Michigan. I think the only tangible reward he ever received for his prodigious labors in working on the bills was to appear in the official picture taken at the signing of the bill in April of 1965 in Governor Romney's office—a small reward for the efforts he expended.

From 1958 to 1964, I introduced a bill into the Senate which would set up a Motor Vehicle Accident Claims Fund, but with no success whatsoever. Two Senators, formerly in the Legislature, Senator Blondy of Detroit and Senator Nichols of Jackson, gave me some encouragement and said they would sponsor my bill. But no other official in Government on the executive level showed any interest.

During this time, a steady flow of letters came in from interested citizens as to what success I might be having in bringing about the passage of the bill. I tried every possible tactic. One year I had a bill based on the New Jersey state plan, another year on the Ontario plan, and a third year on the New York plan. It seemed to make no difference what I tried, there was simply no support for it in the Judiciary Committee of the Senate. I even proposed a bill which would use elements of the plans from all three of the states, and still there was no favorable response. The lobbyists for the auto insurance companies made sure that any bills were bottled up in committee and one year, in a moment of desperation, I paid a personal call on the chairman of the Judiciary Committee of the Senate and asked him what the chances for the bill were. He facetiously said the bill is not only pigeonholed, but it is no longer under consideration. It was not until 1965 that I had renewed hopes for the bill.

Let me give you the chronology of the happenings that year. On

January 6, I issued an annual statement renewing my plea for the establishment of an Accident Claims Fund. On January 26, I filed, with all the members of the Legislature, a detailed plan and recommendation, and much to my surprise I began to get very favorable comments, both from the press and some legislators. The legislative activists who favored the bill were John Bennett, Bill Boos, Marvin Stempien, Joseph Swallow and Donald Holbrook in the House, together with Basil Brown in the Senate. All but John Bennett were attorneys but I was heartened by the fact that Boos, Bennett, Stempien and Brown were Democrats, while Holbrook and Swallow were Republicans. The bill had bi-partisan support. On March 2, I was invited to testify before the House Judiciary Committee and this was the first chance I had been given to appear before a legislative committee in consideration of the bill. I talked about the need for this fund as well as arguing that there were hundreds of thousands of uninsured drivers on the roads. The lobbyists for the auto companies were also present and offered comments in almost direct opposition to everything I said. On May 28, the bill passed the House with recommendation for immediate effect. I was overjoyed, but the bill was still in committee in the Senate. Fortunately, on June 11, the insurance company lobbyists appeared before the Judiciary Committee and admitted that the bill would not hurt their business. Finally, on June 17, the Senate also passed the bill and returned it to the House. I was ecstatic. On June 23, the House officially accepted the Senate's bill and ordered it enrolled which meant, in essence, that it was ready for the Governor's signature.

At lunch that day I met a legislator who said he understood that I was very happy with the success of the bill in both Houses. Then he said, and I think I can quote him correctly, "You think this year all of a sudden the legislators have all become good Christians. That really isn't the reason for the success of your bill." I naturally asked him what he believed was the true reason for the late success and he said, "That bill is going to be a bonanza for the attorneys and they know it." I assured him I did not see that as a possibility since the fund would be established in our office and I did not see that it would be any such bonanza for attorneys. In fact, I suggested that I thought it should run like an insurance company and have most of the claims settled through the adjuster system. His response puzzled me because he laughed heartily and left without further comment.

When I returned to my office, I received an urgent message requesting my presence in Governor Romney's office. When I arrived he immediately said that he was going to have to veto my bill unless I agreed to change one line in it, which would take from me the supervision of attorneys in the operation of the fund and hand them over to the Attorney General's office. This last minute switch certainly amazed me since up to this point neither the Governor nor the Attorney General evinced any interest for the bill. However, he certainly had me over a barrel because I had worked for this bill for eight years. I gave my consent without giving much thought to the situation. However, I pointed out to him that to amend the bill at this late date would allow only one day to have it amended and passed in both the House and the Senate. The Governor's response was very simple. He said, "It can be done." The following day, June 24, the original enrollment was vacated by the House, the bill with one sentence amended was passed by both the House and Senate, and the new bill was again ordered enrolled late that afternoon. It was now ready again for the Governor's signature. I had asked the Governor while I was in conversation with him why he particularly desired this one sentence changed and as I remember our conversation, his only response was, "It is the right thing to do."

The battle for me was not over because the Governor had not made a firm commitment to sign the bill and, on July 14, a group of seven auto insurance firm officials met with him and implored him to veto the bill. In that meeting they charged that it would be "economically and administratively unsound." They predicted that it would develop an "early annual deficit of about six and a half million dollars." These officials labeled the bill as "costly, cumbersome and restrictive." They indicated that they feared being asked to bail out the proposed law if it should run into the red. The bill, as it had passed both houses at that point, would require motorists without insurance to pay a

twenty-five dollar fee when registering their cars, and insured motorists would be charged an additional dollar. The following day,
July 15, I stated that I felt the bill was economically sound and
that I had gone to Ontario to consult with officials there to see if
they felt the changes to be made in the bill were sufficient to keep
it out of the red. They said the Michigan bill was perfectly capable of establishing a financially sound fund. Finally, on July 16,
Governor Romney signed the bill but added that there would be
certain amendments made to eliminate the possibility of the new
fund going into the red.

Immediately after the signing ceremony in the Governor's office,
I started to look for candidates to be director of the fund. I was
able to secure the services of the chief legal counsel of the Michigan Millers Insurance Company of Lansing, Robert Hall, and at
the end of the year he came on the state payroll and worked
prodigiously to organize the administration of the fund. I have always thought that we were very fortunate to secure this man because establishing the fund was a hectic ordeal.

In mid-October the Legislature again amended the law in several ways. One, it changed the minimum claim to be allowed from
fifty to two hundred dollars, and it also raised the charge made to
the uninsured motorist from twenty-five to thirty-five dollars. Both
these changes were efforts to insure the financial solvency of the
fund. I had no opposition to the changes, but in view of the sur-
plus in the fund, the original figure of twenty-five dollars for the
uninsured motorist was probably adequate.

The important change, of course, was the one demanded by the
Governor—the transfer of the attorneys from the State Department payroll to the Attorney General's office. It is interesting to
see how the effect of the change of a single sentence can have far-
reaching effects which, at that time, I neither recognized nor contemplated. A comparison of the original bill to the finally accepted
bill and law, I think, is interesting.

First, the controversial section 26 as originally passed.

Sec. 26. The secretary may employ such office, clerical and professional help as is necessary to carry out the provisions of this act and may contract with such private attorneys and claims investigators as are necessary to defend and investigate all claims and actions against the fund. All wages and professional fees for services hereunder shall be charged to and payable from the fund.

Section 26 as it became the law on June 16, 1965.

Sec. 26. The secretary may employ such office, clerical and professional help and claims investigators as is necessary to carry out the provisions of this act. The attorney general shall assign members of his staff to assist the secretary and may contract with such private attorneys as are necessary to defend actions against the fund. All wages and professional fees for services hereunder shall be charged to and payable from the fund.

After five years of operation of the fund, it is not too early to make an appraisal of its successes and failures, its strengths and weaknesses, and probably to recommend some changes. But first, to talk about its successes. Admittedly, as the godfather of the fund, I may be somewhat prejudiced in its favor. More than ten thousand persons have received payments to compensate for their injuries or property losses since the fund began. These are all people who, if the fund did not exist, would never have received a dime. Second, the fund is paying quite adequately in dollars for bodily injury. The average claim paid for bodily injury in the fiscal year 1969 to 1970 was well over a thousand dollars. This, of course, includes a fair number of full ten thousand dollar payments to persons with extremely serious injuries, as well as persons whose estate made a claim after their death. Third, the fund is making a determined effort to secure repayment from the delinquent motorists involved.

Now, let us look at some of the criticisms that have been made of the fund. First, some people object to the one dollar charge for the insured motorist. As I have said, some insured motorists may be injured as pedestrians and would not be covered by their own insurance. In that case they have recourse to the fund. However, I do not have any objection to the removal of the dollar fee. Second, the assertion has been made that the fund is too expensive to administer. It is now costing almost as much to run the program as the fund is paying in claims. From the beginning until 1970, the fund took in about sixty-seven million dollars, paid almost eleven million dollars in claims, but it cost a little over eleven million dollars to operate. How does this cost compare with that of private insurance companies who are insuring automobiles and drivers? Fortunately we have a means of comparison. The Federal Department of Transportation has been making a two-year study of the auto insurance industry and has some figures on costs. Here is a tabular report taken from the 1971 *Congressional Quarterly*, which indicates that only two-fifths of automobile insurance premiums are paid out in claims.

	Amounts	%
Premiums	$5,768,000,000	100
Company expenses:		
Selling	1,043,386,000	(18)
Overhead	295,374,000	(5)
State taxes	167,817,000	(3)
Total company expenses	1,506,477,000	26
Claim adjusting expenses	798,586,000	14
Claimants' lawyers fees	947,839,000	16
Court costs	111,102,000	2
Total expenses, fees and costs	3,355,004,000	58
Net benefits to claimants	2,412,996,000	42

This comparison cannot be exact; it is something like comparing peaches and plums because the uninsured motorist fund does not have expenses such as selling and state taxes. My feeling is that the operating expenses side of the fund is too large. I believe that it could be trimmed in terms of the amount of money paid out in legal fees. This, of course, was the whole point of Governor Romney's threat to veto the bill if the supervision of attorneys was not turned over to the Attorney General's office. There, of course, they are litigation conscious and will assign an attorney to a claim at the drop of a hat, while I had hoped that attorneys could be replaced, to a much larger degree, by adjusters alone. One situation which brings this about is that about three-fourths of the people who make a claim against the fund do so through an attorney and in such cases the Attorney General always assigns a state attorney, though a private one, to defend the fund. It is to be hoped that in the future more people will recognize they do not need an attorney initially to come in and file a claim, any more than they would if they were going to their own private insurance company.

The Detroit Free Press, on December 29, 1970, pointed out another criticism involving the legal profession. I quote, "The Fund has become a key source of income for specially appointed attorneys, with one state appointed lawyer receiving $51,267 in one year in state paid fees." Another quote from the same article is informative:

> Fund Director Lawrence Carroll says a claimant doesn't really need an attorney, but fund records indicate that 79 percent of all claimants have them.
>
> 'We don't encourage people to bring attorneys in,' Hare says. 'Somehow, word gets around that it is all so complicated. I don't believe that is so.'
>
> The state has its own attorneys who go to court to seek repayment of claims paid. This legal work is handled through the office of Attorney General Frank Kelley, who has parceled out special appointments as fund attorney to 46 lawyers across Michigan, 29 of them in Wayne County.
>
> In 1966, in the fund's first full year of operation, 'some lawyers made a big killing,' Kelley concedes. 'But that's been straightened out and none this year will go beyond the $20,000 to $25,000 range, which is less than the average lawyer makes in private practice.'
>
> In 1968, one of the appointed attorneys, Alan Walt of Southfield, was paid $51,267 by the state, while Michael J. Kelly of Detroit received $34,640, and Richard L. Wolk of Detroit was paid $43,128.

The 46 special assistants appointed by Attorney General Kelley receive $20 an hour for office or field work and $125 a day for courtroom work.

In 1969, Walt was paid $29,267 and Michael Kelly received $16,572. Nathan Conyers of Detroit, brother of U.S. Representative John Conyers, was paid $17,970 as a legal assistant in 1969.

Some well-known outstaters are among the 46 special assistants, including Ray Clevenger of Ann Arbor, a former congressman; John B. Bruff of Mt. Clemens, Democratic candidate for lieutenant governor in 1966; Henry G. Marsh, former mayor of Saginaw, and Thomas Fleming of Jackson, brother and law partner of state Senator James G. Fleming.

In this article the legal rates charged by the private attorneys to the state Government were listed as twenty dollars an hour for office or field work and one hundred and twenty-five dollars a day for courtroom work. Since the time the article was written, those rates have been raised substantially and for the future we can expect that legal costs of defending this fund are going to escalate.

Since the fund was a year old, I have become more and more concerned about the percentage of the total costs that go into legal fees, and from time to time I would follow a specific case just to see what its costs were. One case amassed legal charges of forty-three hundred dollars by the time I had left office at the end of 1970. I suspect the total legal fees will probably approach six thousand dollars. The important question is not whether the attorneys are overcharging for their time and effort, but rather whether a fund can successfully continue to exist when a large portion of its total costs go not to the injured party but to the legal apparatus involved.

To impartially appraise the fund, I think its virtues outweigh its vices and perhaps in this case the end justifies the means. However, I still have one unresolved question in my mind, namely, why did Governor Romney insist on the transfer of the attorneys from the State Department to the Attorney General's office with the threat that he would veto the bill if I objected?

XVII

THE LIGHTER SIDE

THERE were days around the state Capitol when it was fun and games, and one of those days occurred in 1966, when the State Senate gave me a subtle message, but not too subtle. The Democrats in the Senate did not appreciate my approbation for a public disclosure bill and wanted to let me know again of their feelings. The Gongwer News Report gave me their message very succinctly.

A BILL REQUIRING financial disclosures by public officials was unexpectedly plucked from a committee grave in the Senate.

Minority Floor Leader Thomas Schweigert announced yesterday he would move to discharge the State Affairs Committee to get at the bill (S 520).

But even he held little hope for success—until a roll call showed 26 votes for the discharge motion. Twenty votes were needed.

The two lone negative votes were cast by President Pro Tem John T. Bowman and Senator Bernard O'Brien.

Mr. Schweigert's victory was tempered somewhat, however, when Democrats quickly moved the bill from the calendar and into the Appropriations Committee, which was to 'study its financial implications.'

The bill would require annual statements of net worth by any official elected at a statewide election.

That bill is still in study committee five years later. I got the message. The date was April Fool's Day, 1966.

For six years I received an annual visit from a delegation of New York club women who came to ask my help. This was before the age of the Women's Liberation movement, but they were interested in securing a constitutional amendment for the Michigan document guaranteeing equal rights to women. They were a very nice, agreeable, courteous group and I certainly had no objection to the constitutional amendment they proposed. They were willing to give up all the special privileges women have ever had. They were willing to be drafted in time of war; to forgo their dower rights at law; to give up all the industrial standards that give pregnant women special consideration; to accept the responsibility of working late shifts and long hours as men did. But I asked them one question and I was surprised at the answer. My question was, "Do you realize that in a golf tournament the women would have to play off the men's tee instead of their own women's tee, closer to the hole?" The chairman of the delegation spoke up and said "Do you think that's really necessary?" It all depends on what you think is important.

One day an official of the Social Welfare Department gave us a call and remarked that it was strange that over a hundred of those receiving Aid for the Blind also had drivers licenses. This caused confusion in our department and we asked for the names of the persons involved and immediately sent out investigators to each address to determine whether it was possible to be both blind and a driver at the same time. I could see the possible headlines "HARE ALLOWS BLIND DRIVERS ON THE STREET." Our investigation disclosed that it was true that all the hundred persons had drivers licenses, but they had become blind since the time they last received a renewal and their licenses had not yet expired. You can understand I felt relieved. But there was one exception. One man who had tunnel vision could pass the driving sign and reading test, but because of the narrowness of the field of vision he could also qualify for Aid to the Blind. We immediately studied his total record and again I felt relieved to find he had neither convictions for violations nor an accident in his entire driving career.

Irish names are just like gold in political elections. Names like Kelley, Brennan, O'Hara or Cavanaugh (with a C or K) have a great advantage. I think a good recognizable Irish name is worth a hundred thousand votes in a state wide election or a hundred thousand dollars in the campaign fund. One of the most interesting places to test an Irish name is in the Supreme Court races. Here the candidates are nonpartisan and there is no political party designation on the ballot so it becomes name against name. Let us take the case of Paul L. Adams. He had been the Mayor in the Soo and had served a term and a half as Attorney General when Governor John Swainson appointed him to an unexpired term in 1962. However, Adams had to run again in the November election of 1962 against an Irishman, Michael O'Hara. A better Irish name won a close election. However, in April of 1963, Adams ran again. This time against the non-Irish names of Donald Holbrook and Richard Smith. Predictably Adams was more Irish than Holbrook or Smith and therefore became a Supreme Court Justice again and his colleague on the court was O'Hara. Next the luck of the draw reversed itself. Mike O'Hara had to come up for re-election in 1968. This time it brought another Irishman, Thomas Giles Kavanaugh. It was a test of which was the better name and Kavanaugh won with a very narrow victory.

Then there was the case of a disgruntled wife. Her husband had been an employee in a file section of the Driver Licensing Bureau, and as such had access to the records of all drivers. His wife wrote in and testified that over a period of several years he had been removing from the manual files, traffic violation conviction abstracts so that his friends who were getting near the twelve point mark would not be cited. She demanded that he be summarily fired and taken to court and finally ended her letter with the most important facet: he had run off with a younger woman. The problems of security in manual files is always a problem in state Government. Fortunately with the new computer set up it would take a sheer genius to be able to take out a single record from any file. One more plus for electronics.

I had an interesting educational experience at the 1966 Democratic State Convention in Grand Rapids. I went to the convention that year hoping to secure support by resolution from the Democratic Party in my fight for an Implied Consent Law, so that we could better handle the drunk drivers on the highway. I submitted the resolution to the proper committee and hoped for the best. This took place on a Saturday night and very late that evening I received word that the labor caucus was going to oppose my resolution the following morning. I was concerned, but I thought I had an ace in the hole, namely, the Traffic Safety Center of Michigan State University. This department had come into existence in 1957 as a result of the special legislative session of the previous year on traffic safety. I had been much involved in the writing of the program submitted to that special legislative session, so I felt I had a vested interest in its success and, since then, the Traffic Safety Center had done some magnificent pieces of research for me in the safety field. The Director of the department, Gordon Sheehe, had been most cooperative and concerned about traffic safety problems, and most diligent in using the services of the center for very practical solutions to the problem. It was my thought that when the resolution came up for debate on the following Sunday morning, I could get some of the experts from the Safety Center to come to Grand Rapids and testify in behalf of the Implied Consent Law. I called Sheehe and asked him to draft a couple of his best men to make a quick trip to Grand Rapids and prepare to meet the onslaught. He did this and also sent down two excellent research men who were most knowledgeable in the field.

The resolution came up for debate early in the session on Sunday morning and the delegates had spent a hard night in the various caucus rooms where the liquor flowed freely. This tired and irritable group was restless. The two experts from the Traffic Safety Center each gave a fine ten minute presentation supporting the Implied Consent resolution. They talked about how well it had worked in European countries and in other states; about the enormity of the accident problem due to drinking drivers; about the economic costs of accidents; about the ability of a chemical test to determine not only the exact amount of drunkeness on the part of a driver, but also the aid it gave an officer in separating the drunk driver from the person suffering from a nervous disability. In short, it was a fine academic approach. Then Bill Marshall, Secretary-Treasurer of the Michigan AFL-CIO, rose to oppose the resolution. He gave a short but fiery talk and ended it by saying, "How would you like to have a dumb Irish cop pull you out of the car, drag you into the dirty back room of a police station, stick an infected needle in your arm and force you to confess?" The delegates applauded him loudly. When the vote was taken it was approximately five to one opposed to the resolution. Marshall's statements, of course, had been less than factual since the method of testing the alcoholic content of a driver was by the use of a breath test and not by taking blood with a hypodermic needle. Nevertheless, he won the argument. The press asked me to comment on the resolution's defeat and I said I was glad that it was the delegates to the Democratic Convention voting it down rather than the Legislature. Shortly thereafter the Legislature passed an Implied Consent Bill which is in effect now and, I think, working very well. But the lesson I learned from my experience in Grand Rapids was: do not try to sell abstinence and continence to a group of delegates suffering from hangovers.

XVIII

WE ALL MAKE MISTAKES

POLITICIANS, like other members of the human race, do make mistakes. Some of them funny, some of them almost tragic. I have had my share. In the late 1950's one of the Detroit newspapers alleged that I was involved in careless and improper use of manufacturers' plates. These plates are issued to large automotive manufacturers who use them on test cars and in some cases an automobile company may have a thousand or more of these plates, since they test particular segments of that car with experimental parts. But the newspaper discovered that one particular auto company was either allowing or instructing some employees to put the manufacturers' plates on private cars and thus escape paying the usual license plate fee. Quite naturally, our office could not supervise a large automotive company which had twelve hundred plates.

During this period I happened to be driving on Northwestern Highway late one evening when a Cadillac with a manufacturer's plate flashed by me going over eighty miles an hour. I thought to myself, "Aha, this is one of them. I'll follow him right to his door and catch him in the act." I followed him to Orchard Lake Road, he turned east past the Kirk of the Hills Church and then drove off into the winding streets on the north side of Orchard Lake Road. As he swerved from one street to another I thought "He's trying to escape me, or possibly he thinks I am trying to kidnap him." At any rate, after several minutes of following him, he drove into a driveway of a large palatial home and I followed him right to his garage. I got out of the car and said "Don't be afraid, I only want to talk to you." I explained to him that I wanted to know why he had a manufacturer's plate on his new Cadillac limousine. He laughed, raised the hood of the car and pointed out a new experimental carburator and said they were giving it a final test run. He just happened to be Edward Cole, at that time President of Cadillac Motor Car Company and later to become President of General Motors Corporation.

Later, I had another go-around with the General Motors Corporation, with a little different twist. In order to keep undesirable people out of the automobile sales business, we had a rule in the department that before we would license any person to be an automobile dealer, he would have to submit his fingerprints which we would check with the State Police files and, if he had a criminal record, we would deny him the dealership. It so happened that in Flint, Michigan, the Buick Motor Car Company had a factory salesroom which, I believe, listed among its officers the entire hierarchy of the General Motors Corporation. When they applied for their yearly license to be a sales organization, we told them to submit the fingerprints of all the officers of the factory salesroom. It was not long until the legal counsel of the General Motors Corporation gave us a call and said "You can't do that to us. These people are all in *Who's Who of America,* they are the elite of the nation. We can't ask them to be fingerprinted." We had to say, "Sorry, we can't break our regulations for a single dealership, therefore send the fingerprints in." They were not sent. Instead, the dealership reincorporated the factory salesroom. The new officers whose names were submitted and who were fingerprinted were presons much lower in the corporation echelon.

Then there was the case of the "pale-faced plate," a reference to the 1970 colors on the license plate. About ten years ago I thought, in an effort to honor the educational institutions of this state, each year I would use the school colors of some university, and over a period of years I used the yellow and blue of the University of Michigan, the green and white of Michigan State University, the green and gold of Wayne State University, and also colors of several smaller universities in the state. Since the manufacture of license plates is done at Jackson Prison, we must plan color schemes at least two years in advance.

In 1968 Durward B. Varner, the Chancellor at Oakland University, asked if their colors could be used for 1970, since in that year he hoped they would become an autonomous university. We asked him to send in a sample of the school colors and we would give it a try. As soon as we saw those colors, light brown and white, we began to have qualms but we darkened the brown and I asked the Prison Industries to test it to see if it would meet the standard as required by the vehicle code. That standard was that a plate must be readable at one hundred feet in ordinary daylight. The Prison Industries personnel tested the plates and they passed the tests. I, therefore, was not prepared for the complaints from the police authorities who declared that we were endangering the lives of their officers, particularly at a road block when they must stop people coming down the highway. They argued the plates did not have enough contrast in their colors to be visible far enough ahead. By this time, I could see their point, but it was too late. Five million plates had already been manufactured at Jackson Prison. We were stuck with them for a year. The only defense I had for the coloration was, first, it was far better than the standard demanded and, second, in a fair number of states they do not even have a front plate to help the officer at the roadblock. Well, we all make mistakes.

In 1967, I became infatuated with the idea that my State Department should have an Ombudsman. During the last ten years the Ombudsman has appeared in many places throughout the country, but in 1967, there were none in Michigan and I thought it would be a good place to have the first. I designated Gordon Alexander, one of my deputies, to be the Ombudsman and asked him, at least in the beginning, to let me see the complaints and we would see what could be done. After I had named him to the position, the complaints came in quickly but to my shock I found that little could be done about many of them. They tended to be multiple complaints encompassing several departments of Michigan government or county and local city problems. For example, for a few days we were deluged with complaints about automobile liability insurance rates and cancellations of insurance policies. Even though I was the Motor Vehicle Commissioner by statute, I had nothing to do with automobile insurance, the rates or their cancellations, and all we could do was send the complaints to the Insurance Commissioner and hope that he could take some action. In short, I found that an Ombudsman did not work unless the jurisdiction which he covered was large enough to encompass complex complaints. I still think that Michigan could use an Ombudsman covering the entire state government. Unfortunately, for a single department it did not work and I had to withdraw our Ombudsman.

In the late 1950's, I made an intentional mistake, which I never regretted. A woman came to my office with a sad tale. She had been denied a drivers license for eight years due to most unfortunate circumstances. Nine years before, she had been divorced from her husband, but the car which they jointly owned remained titled in both their names. Her husband became involved in a very serious accident and both the husband and wife were jointly sued and a judgment was rendered against them for several thousand dollars, which the husband was unable or unwilling to pay. Subsequently, the husband left the state and the wife remained in Michigan. Since an unpaid judgment was registered against her—even though she had not seen her former husband for several months before the accident took place, she could not drive. Under the Financial Responsibility Law the State Department must revoke the license of any person who has an unpaid judgment against them. I thought eight years off the road for a situation she was not responsible for was far too great a punishment, and I instructed our people to let her take the examination and secure a drivers license as long as she passed the test as required. It was an illegal act but one that I have never regretted. Incidentally, it was the only illegal act that I ever was involved in, at least to the best of my knowledge.

In 1968 I tried my hand at medical research. In that year I read in some of the medical journals that they were finding that certain violent criminals, involved in murders, had a very rare chromosome disorder which was called the XYY male. This particular genetic disorder turned up much more often in the violent murderer type than in the general population. I thought perhaps the incorrigible driver was the victim of this disorder and I put out a press release suggesting that it would be interesting to test a sampling of the very worst drivers in our state and find out whether they had this disorder, and whether this could account for their anti-social behavior. Shortly thereafter, I had a call from Butterworth Hospital in Grand Rapids, and they too were interested in determining whether the very bad and very incorrigible driver could have such a genetic rarity. Finally, we thought that if we could test persons being held in prisons, no matter what offense they committed, if they also had a very bad driving record this would be a fine place to do some research. Gus Harrison, Director of Corrections for the State of Michigan was most cooperative. We supplied him with a list of two hundred inmates who had very bad driving records and he, through his personnel, made contact with them and asked if they would submit to a blood test. They were to be paid two dollars for each blood sample they submitted. This cost was borne by me personally. The medical personnel from Butterworth Hospital went to the Ionia State Hospital to take blood samples and make the tests. Unfortunately for my hopes, not one of the approximately one hundred inmates whose blood was tested showed up with an XYY chromosome so we had to write it off as a good try but a mistaken effort.

A final recital of error was my effort in 1958 to encourage Sunday voting. The previous two years I had been much discouraged with my efforts to encourage higher registration of voters, and indeed to get the already registered out to vote. The statistics indicated about fifty percent of the people registered were voting at elections and only about two-thirds of the eligible people were registered to vote. I had been reading about the very high percentages of the registered voters in other countries participating in elections. In Italy, for instance, over ninety percent of the registered did vote, and other figures, in southern Europe particularly, were comparable. In those countries the voting was done on Sunday. I set up a trial balloon in the form of a press release in the early fall of 1958. The response was almost instantaneous. A flood of letters came in, the majority from Western Michigan, and a high concentration from Kent and Ottawa counties, in extremely strong and almost violent opposition. Sunday is the Lord's day and you must not encourage people to work on that day. I found almost no letters supporting my proposition. Needless to say I dropped the idea and never mentioned it again.

One of my friends, in reading the rough draft of this chapter, suggests I forgot one monumental mistake. That was in running for the governorship in 1960 without the approbation of the UAW.

XIX

MICHIGAN DEMOCRATS:
Why Do They Lose?

AFTER thirty years of active participation in Michigan Democratic politics, twenty at the state administrative level, I have become more and more puzzled by the following question: How can the Democrats ever lose a statewide election?

Three different polls, taken over the past decade by three different poll-takers, indicate that the Democrats should win them all. Every poll indicates that thirty-five to forty percent of Michigan's electorate are hard-line Democrats. Conversely, only twenty to twenty-five percent of the electorate consider themselves rock-ribbed Republicans. This being the case, it would seem that Democrats would encounter a great deal of difficulty in losing statewide elections. But lose they do. In the last ten years, they have managed to lose all four elections for Governor and a seat in the United States Senate.

How can it happen? Why does it happen? The seeming paradox has been particularly intriguing to me, both because of a consuming interest in politics and because I was for sixteen years, as Secretary of State, the state's chief elections officer. As such, I had frequent occasion to study and analyze election returns.

Some obvious, but not wholly rational, answers can be made. One, the polls were wrong. Two, many of the people who were polled did not vote. Three, there was a late shift and people changed their minds just before the election. None of these arguments holds up very well. Polls run by experienced, proven, polling organizations tend to be within two or three percentage points of the actual outcome. Massive, last-minute changes in voters thinking and decisions occur infrequently.

A look at the returns of some of the elections of the last decade deepens the enigma. For instance, how could Democratic Senator Philip A. Hart, in his 1964 bid for re-election to the United States Senate, pile up sixty-four percent of the vote and Neil Staebler, the party's candidate for Governor in the same election, get only forty-three percent. Or, in 1966, how could I get fifty-six percent of the vote in my bid for re-election and Zolton Ferency, the Democratic candidate for Governor, end up with a mere thirty-nine percent. On the surface, it doesn't make sense. Some of the reasons for these discrepancies are fairly evident. Some require closer analysis and some, which I consider significant, are not apparent even to many active Democrats and certainly will draw a sharp counter-fire from certain party activists.

In 1964, Hart was a popular, widely known incumbent, while Staebler was running against the popular, widely known incumbent, Governor George Romney. In 1966, I had the advantage of six terms behind me while Ferency, a relative unknown making his first bid for statewide office, was running against a man being touted for the Republican Presidential nomination.

Conversations I have had with party workers shed a little more light on the question of how Democrats lose statewide elections. A few admitted they were true-blue, down-the-line Democrats only in Presidential election years, fluctuating a bit in other elections. Some have confessed to me that while they think of themselves as solid Democrats, they nevertheless split their tickets on occasion. So, too, do an increasing proportion of the total electorate.

Ask those Democrats why they deviate from the party ticket and a wide variety of answers come forth. One man, a black, told me occasionally voted for Republicans even though he was an officer in his congressional district Democratic organization. Why? Because he did not think the Democrats were particularly sincere on the subject of racial integration. Spelling out his reasoning, he said he had kept track of nineteen prominent Democrats who spoke long, hard and fluently on the need to integrate neighborhoods and schools. Yet, he told me, in their own neighborhoods and schools, only sixteen of the nineteen practiced what they advocated. My check of the list of names he furnished me proved him correct. (Incidentally, two of those he felt were advocating integration and trying to practice it were Detroit Representative William A. Ryan, Speaker of the State House of Representatives, and G. Mennen Williams, during the twelve years he was Governor.)

A rather elderly man of Polish extraction once asserted to me that the Democrats, though vocally concerned with poverty, failed to do anything about it in their personal lives. A retired auto worker, living on a pension, he felt that some of the most prominent, share-the-wealth advocates lived all too well with their multiple homes and three-car garages. He suggested in terse, profane terms that they could improve the poverty situation by sharing some of their own wealth. While conceding that the Republicans dealt no better with the nation's poverty, he said, they at least did not expound so loudly on plans to spread the wealth more evenly. Using that reasoning, he said he would vote for a Ronald Reagan or a Nelson Rockefeller over most Democrats.

A reason frequently voiced for refusing to support Democratic candidates is that party control by labor is too strong and too demanding. Other Democrats, a relatively small number, complain that too many party regulars are primarily bent on getting patronage for themselves and are little concerned with the party program or the basic issues of a campaign. I recall an interesting conversation with a perceptive, long-time Democratic county chairman on the effects and strength of the labor movement within the party. Interestingly, he was a part of the movement himself, being an officer of his labor union. He pointed out that the winning candidate in every Democratic gubernatorial primary in Michigan in the last twenty years had been endorsed by labor. Every State Democratic Party Chairman, he said, had been chosen by labor.

Obviously, there was much truth in his observations. To a fair degree, labor does dominate the party programs and decisions. Its influence is stronger in some years than others. Yet, in the last several years, its domination has substantially declined because of the rising power of the so-called New Left. This rather amorphous, but highly active and increasingly influential, group is taking over much of the power long exercised by labor.

The county chairman-labor official pointed out that the general public does not understand the composition of the AFL-CIO as it operates in Michigan. It is dominated by the United Auto Workers, but it contains other potent, politically active elements. These include the building trades group, of which the county chairman was a member, the steelworkers union and the retail trades union. These and others form a substantial part of the total movement. Since the UAW is the dominant force, however, its members are able to outvote the others and its philosophy prevails. I suspect that the minorities within this labor complex jump parties from time to time simply because of a distaste for the stronger UAW forces.

The objections cited by members of the Democratic Party could not, in my opinion, account for the defection of 250,000 votes, or more, to the Republican column in the gubernatorial elections of 1962, 1964, 1966 and 1970.

Governor John B. Swainson became the first Democratic loser since 1946 when he ran for a second term in 1962 against the Republican challenger, George Romney. Much of the blame for his defeat was ascribed to his veto of the so-called Bowman Bill, a measure named for its chief sponsor, Democratic Senator John T. Bowman of Macomb County. The bill prohibited Detroit from levying its newly enacted income tax on residents of surrounding suburbs who earned their living in Detroit. Needless to say, the measure was highly controversial. Suburbanites working in Detroit favored it overwhelmingly. Detroiters, asserting that commuters should at least pay a portion of what residents paid, knew that the bill would lead to a tax increase in Detroit and speed the exodus of its residents to the suburbs.

Swainson's veto deprived him of much needed support in Oakland

and Macomb counties and in Wayne County, outside of Detroit. Estimates vary, but many observers say that one veto cost him at least 80,000 votes—the margin of Romney's victory.*

Prior to his decision, Swainson called a meeting of the Democratic Party's leadership group to discuss the bill. He told them that while he had qualms about it, he was going to put his signature on the bill. For several hours, party leaders talked over every aspect of the bill and all its possible ramifications. While a few opposed Swainson's reasoning, I think everyone in the room agreed that, from the political viewpoint, it was wise to accept the bill.

The next day, to my utter surprise, I heard a radio broadcast announcing that Swainson had vetoed the bill. My immediate reaction was "Good Lord, somebody is trying to defeat him!" Rumor circulated that the overnight switch resulted from a meeting between the Governor and a top-ranking UAW official who persuaded him to take the veto route. That official, if such was the case, has never been publicly identified.

Regardless, Swainson's decision helped seal his defeat, notwithstanding his adoption of the stirring campaign slogan "The Courage to Do What is Right" and the upturn of Democratic fortunes in the latter days of the campaign.

The 1964 election was the year of the Barry Goldwater candidacy and the political situation differed greatly from 1962. Early in the year it became fairly obvious that Goldwater was going to win the Republican Presidential nomination. It soon became equally obvious that he was taking some very unpopular political positions. One that hurt him severely, his opposition to the Social Security Act, generated widespread fear among the millions of Americans who were collecting social security payments or who had hopes of receiving them. At any rate, the Goldwater candidacy did nothing for the Republican Party. In Michigan, it did nothing for Romney, who was running for re-election against Neil Staebler, former Democratic State Chairman

---

* *The Politics of Change in Michigan,* Carolyn Steiber, Michigan State University Press, 1970. p. 53.

and then Michigan's Congressman-at-Large. To all of us on the Democratic ticket, it appeared that a political bonanza was coming our way. As early as mid-August, we saw that the entire ticket might be elected.

Until then, Romney had taken several verbal potshots at me. Most of them backfired or failed to create any stir. With one, particularly hilarious to me, he contended that I had no particular interest in traffic safety, despite my continuing efforts and public statements over the years as Chairman of the State Safety Commission. All this, Romney said, was mere political gadgetry. I countered that Romney, if he were truly interested in traffic safety himself, would have attended at least one meeting of the Commission, of which he was a member. He had not shown up at a single meeting during his two years in office.

A second Romney salvo charged that I didn't know much about my job because the vehicle license plates issued annually by my office were getting rusty. That was an easy one to field. I said simply that the plates were made by Prison Industries at Southern Michigan Prison in Jackson, which was under his supervision and control. The blame for rusting plates thus fell much closer to his home than where he was trying to place it. Finally, I suggested that if he were unable to improve the quality of license plates he should turn over supervision of the prison to my department. That ended the campaign argument on rusty plates.

Romney was equally aware of the Republican's deteriorating position, and the polls showed it. He immediately began to separate himself from the Goldwater philosophy and, generally, from the Republican Party. By the beginning of October, it was evident that he, and his obvious presidential ambitions, might be in serious trouble.

Early in the month, I received a strange telephone call from Romney's office, one floor up from mine in the Capitol. The Governor said he would like to see me and talk over the campaign situation. I had no idea what he had in mind. The explanation came as soon as he walked into my office with his administrative aide, Walter DeVries. Quickly and bluntly, Romney declared that he would not mention my name for the rest of the campaign, if I would do likewise with him. Without saying so, he was trying to silence one person who could do damage to his campaign for re-election.

Once he stated his case, Romney's mission was clear. I was strongly favored in my own bid for re-election and Romney had personally persuaded Allison Green, then Speaker of the House of Representatives, to run against me. In return, the Governor had promised to campaign strongly for Green. He did so, right up to the moment that he walked into my office.

The meeting in my office ended in agreement that neither of us would mention the other in public appearances for the rest of the campaign. I had never in previous campaigns ever mentioned my opposition. The victim, of course, was Green, a fine candidate with a good record, whose biggest weakness was inadequate identity with the voters. He badly needed to become better known. Romney, however, had clearly decided that Green must be sacrificed to assure his own re-election. This teetotaling, former auto company president and church leader, downgraded by many seasoned politicians as a naive, Johnny-come-lately to the political wars, was a shrewd and sharp operator in many respects, a man who knew what he wanted and how to get it.

Neil Staebler, on the other hand, was campaigning for the governorship at a pedestrian pace. Early in the campaign I had the feeling that he was relying on a tidal wave of Democratic votes to carry him in with the rest of the ticket.

I had occasion to hear what Staebler had to say at a couple of campaign affairs and I was amazed. He made a good and brave statement at the Ionia Free Fair about raising the standards for meat inspection. Many farmers in that rural area of central Michigan butchered and sold their beef and Staebler's position did not go over with them. I heard many speak rather bitterly about his views.

At a meeting of foundry workers in Muskegon, Staebler again voiced his position on raising standards for meat packers. He said he recognized that meat prices would rise but asserted the cost would be well worth it. After the meeting, the foundry workers grumbled to me, and to each other, that they were not prepared to pay higher prices.

I was surprised that a man of Staebler's experience, a former state party chairman and Democratic national committeeman, was apparently picking out unpopular positions and ramming them home in the very places where they would do the most damage to his campaign. Privately, I wondered whether he was trying to defeat himself. Certainly, with the political tides flowing in favor of the Democrats, he had a grand and glorious opportunity to win election.

The results were a disaster for Staebler. He lost to Romney by more than 400,000 votes while I was defeating Green by about 800,000 votes. (Romney, probably to atone for his go-it-alone tack with Green, later appointed him acting Auditor General and then State Treasurer.)

The gubernatorial campaign of 1966 was a re-run of the 1964 campaign, only worse from the Democratic point of view. Romney, running for a third term, had, by then, had four years to solidify his organization. He had become a national figure with a good possibility of entering the presidential sweepstakes two years later. The Democratic candidate, Zolton Ferency, was not widely known outside the party and had never held an elective public office. He was further handicapped by his inability to raise the large sums of money needed to wage a good campaign and had difficulty putting together a strong campaign apparatus. He worked hard and showed himself an extremely formidable speaker in a political context. His severe handicaps, however, made it a foregone conclusion, early in the campaign, that he was not going to win.

Ferency's wit and slashing style sometimes did him damage. He hurt himself on one occasion when he appeared on the same platform with Romney, at a meeting of the Michigan Municipal League. Ferency unleashed a highly personal, vitriolic attack on the Governor and his record. The vehemence of his assault repelled many listeners and without doubt contributed to his defeat.

The results of the race were thoroughly disheartening to the Democrats. Romney piled up slightly more than sixty percent of the vote. Ferency's thirty-nine percent was the lowest mark for the Democrats since the Republican heydays of the 1920's. In the same election, Robert Griffin, appointed to the United States Senate by Romney after the death of Democrat Patrick McNamara that spring, upset G. Mennen Williams in the Senate contest. Attorney General Frank Kelley and I came through with rather substantial victories. Nevertheless, the loss of the race for Governor left a large vacuum in Democratic ranks. Once again, there was no one with the authority to pull the party together and impose some necessary discipline on the dissidents.

The campaign year 1970 opened auspiciously for the Democrats. It was apparent by spring that President Richard Nixon could not get the sagging economy turned around and that by November the nation would be suffering both from inflation and high unemployment. Both situations favored the Democratic candidates.

Four Democrats ran in the primary for Governor. The winner was State Senator Sander Levin, a former state party chairman and the candidate endorsed by the United Auto Workers. He won a clear-cut victory over Ferency, Macomb County Prosecutor George Parris and State Representative George F. Montgomery. Interestingly, two of the best possibilities as vote-getters, Jerome Cavanaugh, former Mayor of Detroit, and Frank Kelley, had not been considered by the labor hierarchy for endorsement.

Republicans nominated Governor William G. Milliken, who had moved up from Lieutenant Governor when Romney joined the Nixon cabinet early in 1969. His only opponent was a little known, muckraking publisher from Howell, James Turner.

The first real sign of trouble for the Democrats was the poor showing in the voter registration drive. Two years earlier, some 500,000 new voters were registered between July and October. In contrast, only 120,000 new registrations were recorded in the same period of 1970. Worse yet was the tally in heavily Democratic Wayne County, where only 17,000 new voters were registered, about one-tenth the number who signed up in the July-October period of 1968. It was all too apparent that the nuts and bolts of the party organization were not functioning.

Another warning sign appeared at the Democratic state convention in August. Amid some confusion, the convention adopted a resolution urging amnesty for draft dodgers. The candidates, caught off guard, did not reject it until the next day, after the action had made headlines across the state.

A third development at the convention caused little public comment but a good deal of soul-searching by some of the voters. This was the composition of the Democratic ticket. The twelve man ticket had not been assembled in accordance with the established practice of trying to attract voters of all faiths and racial and ethnic backgrounds. Three of the candidates were Jews, three were blacks and five were Catholics. The ticket contained only one WASP. While no one, including the newspapers, made public note of the unbalanced ticket, I heard grumblings, particularly from Protestant church groups having political action committees.

Also working against the Democrats was an ill-concealed rift between party leaders and the Secretary of State Branch Managers Association. Forming the Association are some two hundred branch managers appointed by the Secretary of State, whose earnings are derived principally from fees collected from the sale of license plates. Some branches are quite lucrative, others much less so. This group has contributed large sums to the state party campaigns—in fact, a million dollars in the last twelve or thirteen years.

When I announced in September, 1969, that I would not run for re-election, the branch managers' first concern, naturally, was the choice of my successor and how they could back him in the election. At the same time, State Democratic Chairman James McNeely called on them to contribute money to the party as they had done in the past. Their donations amounted to as much as $100,000 in any one political year, as the economical campaigns I had waged over the years permitted them to make large contributions. I never spent more than $18,000 in any of my seven campaigns and the expenses for my first campaign in 1954 amounted to only $5,400.

The Branch Managers Association, knowing full well that a first-time candidate for Secretary of State would need a great deal of money to build statewide identification with the voters, rejected McNeely's request for funds. They said they intended to spend their money to help elect a candidate who would assure them of retention of their jobs if he won the election. The Democratic State Central Committee was highly upset. They had come to expect the branch managers to finance from one-fourth to one-third of the Committee's annual budget. After an exchange of letters between McNeely and Charles Deamud, chairman of the Branch Managers Association, the situation deteriorated badly. In January, 1970, officers of the State Central Committee adopted the following resolution:

> It was the unanimous decision that the chairman of the party would meet with the county and district chairmen and other key local Democratic leaders and inform them that the party expected that the assessment levied on themselves through the Branch Managers Association be remitted directly to the state party, and to then be divided with the county district organization by May, 1970. If the remittance is not made by May 1, it is pledged that the party will demand of the Democratic nominee for Secretary of State a commitment to remove on January 1, 1971, all those failing to comply.

The resolution, instead of ending the dispute, polarized the differences between the party and the branch managers. Association members looked upon the party's ultimatum as a kind of political extortion, with their jobs at stake. Beyond that, they had heard that Senator Hart, running for re-election, had built a campaign fund of his own far bigger than anything they could raise and had refused to turn over any excess to the party. In fact, Hart was so well financed he was able to invest part of his funds in United States Treasury Certificates against the day the funds were needed.

The situation went from bad to worse, with recriminatory letters going back and forth between the Association and the party leadership. It came to a head in April when McNeely asked my representative and chief deputy in Detroit, Walter Elliott, to leave a party leadership meeting and not to reappear at any in the future. I made no public mention of my expulsion and that of the Branch Managers Association from party leadership meetings. Both the Association and I wanted to preserve at least the illusion of unity, and we could see that the Republicans were in vast disarray. The GOP was fighting its internal battles in public, thus enhancing the chances of a Democratic victory in November.

Personally, I strongly suspected that party leaders, in removing me from their councils, were not solely concerned with the loss of $100,-000 in contributions. It was my feeling that they did not want either me or representatives of the branch managers sitting at the table when they were discussing policy matters.

In the end, the Democratic Party did give the impression of substantial unity and a highly satisfactory candidate, Richard Austin of Detroit, was nominated for Secretary of State at the party's August convention. Members of the Branch Managers Association immediately asked him: "Will you fire us January 1, 1971?" He responded: "I will not commit myself to anyone or any party to hire or to fire any person, and I shall only be a candidate under those circumstances."

Still, the combination of weaknesses—poor voter registration results, the draft-dodger resolution, the unbalanced ticket, the intra-party warfare involving the branch managers—did their damage. Without them, Sander Levin, the only defeated Democratic candidate for statewide office, would almost certainly have defeated Milliken. As it was, he closed the gap substantially from the opening days of the campaign and lost by a mere 44,000 votes.

The Milliken victory was a minor political miracle. The Detroit News (5–16–71) described it as follows:

In the dozen states of Middle America—Michigan, Ohio, Indiana, Illinois, Wisconsin, Minnesota, Iowa, Kansas, Missouri, North Dakota, South Dakota, and Nebraska—there were

17 major elections for Governor and U.S. Senate in 1970.

These states comprise the Republican heartland and all but two, Michigan and Hubert Humphrey's Minnesota, were carried by Nixon in his 1968 presidential campaign. But in 1970 the GOP won only four of the 17 races in these states and in each case by the smallest of margins—51 percent.

Three of the four winners were well known Republicans running in predominantly Republican states: Robert A. Taft in Ohio, Senator Roman Hruska in Nebraska, and incumbent Robert Ray, of Iowa.

The fourth winner was Milliken. In a strongly Democratic state, and despite a recession economy, a Democratic sweep of all other state offices, a GOP Senate candidate who could pull only a third of the vote, and a position in favor of three major issues rejected by the voters (parochiaid, housing bonds, and the vote for 18 year-olds) Milliken still pulled out a victory.

The loss of four straight elections for Governor—by candidates Swainson, Staebler, Ferency and Levin—dealt a series of body blows to the party organization. Control of the Governor's chair is absolutely essential for operation of a strong, cohesive political party. The Governor has the power of appointment and the power of political patronage, key factors in organizing a party. More than that, he has a platform and a public forum to speak from and mold the issues that the party espouses. A party can win legislative majorities and capture other statewide offices, but those do not make up for the loss of the governorship.

Again, I pose the question: Why do the Democrats, in a state where Democrats predominate, consistently lose this key race? It is even more perplexing in view of John Kennedy's victory over Nixon in 1960, Lyndon Johnson's over Goldwater in 1964 and Hubert Humphrey's over Nixon—in Michigan—in 1968. This leads to speculation as to whether certain influential individuals, or indeed a group or groups, are determined to make sure that the Democrats do not take over the Governor's office, no matter how well they do in other election contests.

It is by no means unheard of for powerful elements within a political party to be content without a governor, or even to prefer having one of the opposition party in office. Carolyn Steiber, in her book, *The Politics of Change in Michigan**, recalls such a situation with Michigan Republicans during the G. Mennen Williams era in the 1940's and 1950's.

A more likely source of tension is the state legislature, which, in the view of several seasoned observers, themselves Republican, never welcome having a governor of their own party in command. At such times, the opportunities to obstruct are less and the risks are greater, compared to the publicity, bathed in a virtuous light, that can be gained from obstructing a governor of the opposite party. Since the American governmental process draws its legislators and executives from different constituencies, the possibility of cooperative action is always limited. In Michigan, this inherent difference in viewpoint was compounded by party differences as well. The legislature, which strongly tended to be Republican, may have enjoyed the Williams years immensely. Then it was possible to block the progress of a very popular Democratic governor, and virtually any opposition legislator was assured of a headline.

'When the GOP power base was in the legislature,' said one Republican, 'they didn't care if they *never* got a Republican Governor.'

The contrast is startling between the ferocity of the battles for control of the state Democratic party, particularly the state chairman's post, and the tepid support given some of its candidates for governor. Two groups within the party have, in common, a fierce desire for control of the party without being overly interested in electing a Democratic Governor. Both are rather small but, because they tend to be in the ranks of party leaders, they are important. The first contains those who are reaping financial benefits in political patronage which, under a Democratic administration, would be channeled to a greater degree through the Governor's office. Examples are

* *The Politics of Change in Michigan,* Carolyn Steiber, Michigan State University Press, 1970. pp. 98–99.

the branch managers, attorneys appointed by the Attorney General and recipients of judicial appointments, such as receiverships. All are doing well enough so that they are in no hurry to change the political power line-up.

The second group has had many names but might collectively be called the New Left. The present aggregation came formally into being in 1967 as the Michigan Conference of Concerned Democrats (MCCD). Over the next two years, its adherents gradually became known as the New Democratic Coalition (NDC).

Considering their numbers, no more than a few hundred, they exert a tremendous impact on the Democratic Party. Mrs. Steiber takes note of this in her book:

> When the Michigan Democrats met in Detroit's Cobo Hall early in 1969, there was enough strength, led by the New Democratic Coalition, to push through an anti-Vietnam resolution, as well as anti-parochiaid and pro-abortion reform measures. Two new party officers were chosen from the rebel ranks to sit on the party's executive board, and the presence of dissenters in all the party councils is now a fact of life with the Democrats.*

In August of 1970, the NDC gave more evidence of their strength and organizational effectiveness when, with perhaps twenty percent of the delegate strength, they pushed through, on the convention floor, the resolution recommending amnesty for draft evaders. The candidates repudiated it the next day. Had it been allowed to stand for as long as a week, the whole ticket would have been seriously hurt.

NDC members, in general, are quite different from the typical person active in the political world. Few are seekers of patronage or job hunters in any way. Most are dedicated, primarily, to curing the social evils of the country and are convinced that it can be accomplished only by changing the state and national political leadership. Indeed, they are nearly all intent on doing away with the present establishment, whatever that may be.

Ibid. p. 108.

Their influence is not likely to wane. They are dedicated to their cause. They are bolstered by the fact that state government, as it is structured in Michigan, cannot adequately cope with the social ills the New Left wants to remedy—the failures of the penal and welfare systems, the plight of migrant workers, racial and campus disorders. It is not because of the way political parties are organized, or because of individual failures or shortcomings, that government cannot adequately deal with such problems. The basic reason—and I realize the import of this statement—is that the three elements of government, as they are established in the State Constitution, tend to counteract each other. Any of the three branches—Executive, Legislative or Judicial—can exercise the veto power over the other two to a degree greater than the "Checks and Balances" system intended them to do. The net result is that the *status quo,* or something near to it, remains and no great gains are registered in efforts to solve the worst of our social problems.

Some of the most prominent activists in the NDC are Zolton Ferency, Congressman John Conyers of Detroit, State Senator and Democratic National Committeeman Coleman Young of Detroit and former State Senator Roger Craig of Dearborn. The group made their first substantial show of strength at the 1968 Democratic National Convention in Chicago. Nearly all strongly and enthusiastically backed Senator Philip Hart in his support of Senator Eugene McCarthy for the presidency. When McCarthy later refused to support the party nominee, Hubert Humphrey, the NDC took little further part in the political councils of the convention.

The NDC chairman is Alvin Fishman, a Detroiter little known outside party ranks but long active in political affairs. He is a very presentable, a most articulate and highly intelligent person. His long background in the leftist movement has given him valuable experience in party organization and manipulation. His left wing convictions have not come to him overnight. As long ago as 1950 he was actively promoting the Communist inspired Stockholm Peace Pledge and more lately he has been active in the Michigan Conference of Concerned Democrats and helped found the New Democratic Coalition.

He has also been active in the Detroit based Urban Alliance—a left wing organization whose main function is to rate political candidates.

What lies ahead for Michigan's New Left movement?

I would guess their next move will be to try to take over the leadership of the Democratic Party. All over the world, the pattern for this type of group is to move into political organizations and attempt to take over. With their hard-working corps of workers, they just might succeed in Michigan, though their tactics might impel them to lose some elections. Even standing at the party helm, it is not likely they would raise their hands and proclaim they belong to the radical left. Their strategems would more likely take the form of declarations of concern for Michigan's overwhelming social problems and their determination to solve them.

There would be no immediate, drastic stands on troublesome issues. But certain positions characteristic to left-wing movements would soon show up. The leftist leadership can be expected to raise strong, continuous protest against both the police and the courts, although in fairness it must be acknowledged that the police system is far from perfect and that the long delays in court processes are often justice denied. They will agitate for an immediate end of the military draft and amnesty for draft evaders. They will work towards the infiltration of college administrations and for the abolition of college-based military research and any anti-ballistic missile system. They will support unilateral disarmament and any position tending to criticize the government establishment.

On the other hand, they rarely offer criticism for actions taken by Iron Curtain nations. It was significant that they did not join in the public outcry in November, 1970, when a Lithuanian sailor who leaped aboard a U.S. Coast Guard vessel, seeking refuge in the United States, was turned back to Soviet crewmen and forceably returned to his ship.

They will look for attractive, charismatic candidates to support, particularly any who are not too stable emotionally. I fear the pattern of 1968 will be repeated, with support rallying around the kind of person Senator Eugene McCarthy showed himself to be in Chicago

—far less than a sturdy oak in the Democratic forest.

To bring all these changes about, the New Left will encourage young people on the campuses to take positions of violent opposition. Confrontation will be the order of the day. Without doubt, they will create chaos in the Democratic Party in their moves to take control. One tactic, used by any group attempting to assume command, is to take over the party's internal voting mechanisms. The recent imposition of "proportional voting" procedures for selecting members of the Michigan Democrats' county executive committees is a move in that direction.

Proportional representation is a voting method first proposed by another Hare, a third cousin of mine, in the 1850's. It is based on a theory that minority interests, opinions and party affiliations should be represented rather than geographical areas. Before he died, Hare refuted the system and admitted that it tends to divide the electorate, create splinter parties and make less certain the establishment of a responsible and durable governing body. Experience with proportional representation in Europe in the last half century and in the New York City Common Council, which cast it out years ago, indicate both the unrepresentative nature of the selected candidates and the chaos the system creates. That is more than likely to be the case with the Democrats' executive committees.

Outside the party, the New Left probably will try by every means possible to bring disrepute on our election methodology, hoping to raise public doubts about the integrity of the voting system. Loss of confidence in the method of choosing public officials would be a long step forward to the group's ultimate goals.

I realize that these strong judgments on the left-wing, and the admittedly alarming predictions of how they will try to take control, will raise some cries of "foul." My only reply is to counsel patience, and a wait-and-see attitude by every alert citizen. I think the passage of five years will demonstrate the truth of my allegations and make more evident some of the reasons why Michigan Democrats, though numerically stronger than the Republicans, often have trouble winning statewide elections.

XX

I REST MY CASE

HISTORY records that no form of government or culture endures forever. The Roman Empire, the Greek City States and even the Ptolemy Dynasty in Egypt which endured for several centuries finally passed out of existence. They did not perish over night but the signs of disintegration were apparent many years before their demise. For one thing, the collapse followed when their citizens no longer had confidence in their government and would not support it, and when that government could no longer solve the problems of its people.

I feel that the American Republic, after less than two centuries of existence, is beginning to show these signs of disintegration. I cannot believe that the American people of the 1770's and 1870's were fundamentally different from those of the 1970's but certainly the attitude of the citizenry toward its government has changed completely. Rather than blaming the people, their leaders or their political parties, I would place the majority of the blame on the rigid governmental organization of the state. It is almost unchanged for close to two centuries and simply is not responding quickly and effectively to the needs of the people—nor can it because of its rigidity.

My suggestions and examples throughout this book have illustrated this breakdown. In the various chapters I have promoted several themes. First, that we must have a stronger central executive office in Michigan, and the Governor must not only be given greater powers, but in return he must take greater responsibility. Secondly, I recommend a reformation within the legal profession even though they may protest that this is an encroachment into a private affair. But they are not truly a private profession, they are in reality a part of the trinity of government. It is the attorneys who are members of the judiciary and, indeed, of our Supreme Court. They are the Prosecuting Attorneys of the counties and the Attorney Generals of the state. They are the Judiciary Committees of the Legislature and the single greatest force in state government. Their public image must be improved and they must regain the confidence of the Michigan people. Third, I advocate that the slow and cumbersome Grand Jury system be at least partially replaced by the Ombudsman concept. Certainly one of the great flaws of our government is the inability of the average man to secure redress from what he believes to be evils perpetrated by officialdom in state government. Fourth, the fetish for privacy on the part of public officials must end. The concealment of facts from the citizenry is indefensible. Those people who are the beneficiaries of the public tax system must reveal more of the facts than they do at present. I have particularly pointed out the facts about slush funds and political patronage, because these are two of the so-called unmentionables in the political climate. Finally, a real effort to bring about both economy and efficiency in government can only come with two giant steps: to define the goals to be achieved through large expenditures of money, and to encourage the local governments and local citizenry to act for themselves rather than to encourage a burgeoning political bureaucracy.

How serious is this situation? In my opinion it is later than most people know. I would not predict that revolution is in the immediate future, but I would predict that if we do not make changes within the next decade the increasing population pressures will cause some kind of an explosion. Government may stay on its present course, but if a majority or even one-third of the citizenry who are activists decide that it is an intolerable situation they will move for a dictatorial leadership that can get things done.

What chance is there for the reforms I advocate? Any change would be dependent upon the forces that control government. I have mentioned some of them: the labor movement, the lobbyists, the legal profession, the chambers of commerce, the news media and, hopefully, the common man on election day. Unfortunately, many of these forces in molding government are satisfied with the *status quo*. The structural organization of government has been favorable to them and is enriching them perhaps in prestige, power or money, and they have little incentive to bring about change. But one thing for sure, if there is no reform the day shall come when there will be a violent upheaval by the "have nots" and that is one thing I would not wish to anticipate. I rest my case.

A NOTE OF THANKS

I cannot conclude this book without giving special thanks to a group of attorneys who have been most helpful to me over a long period of years. I have already mentioned my debt to Professor Harold Norris of the Detroit College of Law. In Lansing, Thomas Downs was most helpful in explaining the intricacies of the Workman's Compensation Law, and Thomas Walsh kept me up to date concerning the progress of driver education in the Lansing School District. In Detroit, Hy Kramer was most helpful in the technicalities of handling the funding of political campaigns. In Livingston County, the Prosecuting Attorney, Thomas Kizer Jr., helped me by explaining the problems of traffic safety on the rural county level. Chuck MacLean, in Lansing, was a diligent researcher in digging out the legal canons relating to "Public Disclosure," as it affects attorneys. On the Grand Jury Level, two judges impressed me a great deal, one, Chester O'Hara, who conducted the State Fair Grand Jury in the early 1950's, and Judge George Bowles, whose Grand Jury in 1967 involved election and campaign procedures. Finally, I must mention the fine work done by my own deputy, Jack Dodge, in the years between 1957 and 1961. He came to me from the office of Dean Acheson's firm in Washington, at a substantial financial sacrifice to work for the state.

In an earlier chapter, I have said that there are virtues to both a patronage system and a Civil Service system, and I must give special recognition to five civil servants who worked long and diligently for me. They were my secretaries over a period of twenty years. First was Marie Orr, at the State Fair from 1952 to 1954. Then, in the Secretary of State's office, June Foster, Beverly Goulding, Catherine Haughton and Mary George.